# Test-Driven Python Development

Develop high-quality and maintainable Python applications using the principles of test-driven development

**Siddharta Govindaraj**

BIRMINGHAM - MUMBAI

# Test-Driven Python Development

First published: April 2015

Production reference: 1210415

Published by Packt Publishing Ltd.
Livery Place
35 Livery Street
Birmingham B3 2PB, UK.

ISBN 978-1-78398-792-4

www.packtpub.com

Cover image by Jayanand Govindaraj (jayanand@gmail.com)

# Credits

**Author**
Siddharta Govindaraj

**Reviewers**
Sharad Bagri
Kevin Davenport
Vivek Vidyasagaran
Devesh Chanchlani
Dorai Thodla
Kiran Gangadharan
Cees de Groot
David Simick
Fernando Ramos
Christopher Humphries

**Commissioning Editor**
Julian Ursell

**Acquisition Editor**
Nikhil Karkal

**Content Development Editor**
Sumeet Sawant

**Technical Editor**
Ruchi Desai

**Copy Editors**
Vikrant Phadke
Sameen Siddiqui
Alpha Singh

**Project Coordinator**
Danuta Jones

**Proofreaders**
Simran Bhogal
Stephen Copestake
Safis Editing
Paul Hindle

**Indexer**
Mariammal Chettiyar

**Graphics**
Jason Monteiro

**Production Coordinator**
Arvindkumar Gupta

**Cover Work**
Arvindkumar Gupta

# About the Author

**Siddharta Govindaraj** first encountered Python in 2002, and it has remained his favorite programming language ever since. He was an early participant in BangPypers, India's first Python community, and a speaker at InPycon. He is the founder of Silver Stripe Software, an Indian product start-up that develops products based on Python. A vocal proponent of the language, Siddharta extols the virtues of Python to anyone who will listen — and also to those who won't. His blog is at http://www.siddharta.me.

# Acknowledgments

Abhaya Shenoy, my colleague at Innvo Systems, introduced me to Python back in 2002. I spent a month working with Python, and then I was hooked to it for life. I was also introduced to test-driven development in 2002. Thanks to Moses Hohman, who worked for ThoughtWorks at that time.

I would like to thank all the reviewers for their participation: Sharad Bagri, Kevin Davenport, Vivek Vidyasagaran, Devesh Chanchlani, Dorai Thodla, Kiran Gangadharan, Cees de Groot, David Simick, Fernando Ramos, and Christopher Humphries.

Devesh Chanchlani and Dorai Thodla spent a number of hours reviewing the book with me and offering valuable suggestions. Sharad Bagri, Kevin Davenport, and Vivek Vidyasagaran also provided a ton of feedback that helped the book become what it is.

Mohammad Fahad and Ruchi Desai from Packt Publishing did a great job coordinating with a number of people and getting this book in shape.

A special shout-out to the Python community! One of the reasons I love Python is not only the language but also the awesome community around it.

Finally, I would like to thank my family. This book could not have been completed without their constant encouragement, motivation, and support.

# About the Reviewers

**Sharad Bagri** is a passionate software developer, adventurer, and an inquisitive learner. His first date with Python happened during the New Year break of 2013, and he fell in love with it. Ever since then, he can be seen cajoling his fellow programmers to try Python. He is a seasoned programmer and has worked with various languages and technologies.

Sharad secured his MS degree in computer engineering from Virginia Tech, USA. His research focused on verification of electronic circuits, which resulted in several papers published in peer-reviewed international conferences. Before going to Virginia Tech, he worked at Qualcomm and ABB in the embedded software and hardware development departments. He completed his bachelor's degree in electronics and communication engineering (ECE) from National Institute of Technology (NIT), Nagpur, India, where he was involved in diverse projects related to robotics, programming, and embedded systems development. His interests also include reading, running, cycling, and filmmaking.

**Kevin Davenport** is a senior technical program manager at Amazon.com, working on scalable solutions for offer recommendations and comparisons. He has 10 years of experience in statistical and machine learning implementations, systems engineering, and product management. Other than work, Kevin enjoys sharing his ideas on his blog (http://kldavenport.com/) and volunteering for Washington's Evergreen Mountain Bike Alliance.

> I would like to thank the author of this book for articulating a compelling case for test-driven development and the use of Python. Many thanks to Packt Publishing for the opportunity to contribute to this publication and for their contributions to the open source world.

**Vivek Vidyasagaran** is pursuing his master's degree at Carnegie Mellon University's Entertainment Technology Centre, where he works on developing the next generation of digital entertainment. He completed his bachelor's degree in computer science and engineering from VIT University, Vellore, India. Currently, he works on game design and development. Python has been an important tool in his development toolbox and he has been using it to create games and apps since 2010. Vivek is also very interested in the core technologies behind modern entertainment, such as computer graphics, GPU computing, and game engines.

# www.PacktPub.com

## Support files, eBooks, discount offers, and more

For support files and downloads related to your book, please visit www.PacktPub.com.

Did you know that Packt offers eBook versions of every book published, with PDF and ePub files available? You can upgrade to the eBook version at www.PacktPub.com and as a print book customer, you are entitled to a discount on the eBook copy. Get in touch with us at service@packtpub.com for more details.

At www.PacktPub.com, you can also read a collection of free technical articles, sign up for a range of free newsletters and receive exclusive discounts and offers on Packt books and eBooks.

https://www2.packtpub.com/books/subscription/packtlib

Do you need instant solutions to your IT questions? PacktLib is Packt's online digital book library. Here, you can search, access, and read Packt's entire library of books.

## Why subscribe?

- Fully searchable across every book published by Packt
- Copy and paste, print, and bookmark content
- On demand and accessible via a web browser

## Free access for Packt account holders

If you have an account with Packt at www.PacktPub.com, you can use this to access PacktLib today and view 9 entirely free books. Simply use your login credentials for immediate access.

# Table of Contents

# Preface

Today, organizations encounter an ever-increasing delivery frequency problem. The days of delivering a new version every few years are long gone. The test-driven development process enables individuals and teams to deliver code that is not only robust but maintainable as well. Combine this with the rapid development speed of the Python language and you have a combination that enables the delivery of new features at the pace demanded by the market.

*Test-Driven Python Development* covers the end-to-end unit testing process, from the first simple test to complex tests that involve multiple components and interactions.

## What this book covers

*Chapter 1, Getting Started with Test-Driven Development*, is the introductory chapter. It eases you into the TDD process by setting the context of why we need TDD and quickly getting started with a test.

*Chapter 2, Red-Green-Refactor – The TDD Cycle*, goes deeper into the TDD process, driving the implementation of our example project as we write more tests.

*Chapter 3, Code Smells and Refactoring*, explores common types of smelly code, and we go back to our example project and clean up the smells we find. A key benefit of TDD is that it provides a safety net so that we can go in and clean up messy code.

*Chapter 4, Using Mock Objects to Test Interactions*, shows the use of mocking to implement the parts of our example project that depend on other systems. How do you test code that depends on external subsystems? We answer that question here by introducing mock objects.

*Chapter 5, Working with Legacy Code,* is about the fact that we often need to clean up or add features to old code that doesn't have existing tests. This chapter looks at strategies for doing this by working through one of the modules in our sample application.

*Chapter 6, Maintaining Your Test Suite,* proves that unit tests are also code and good coding practices apply to test code as well. This means keeping them well organized and easy to maintain. This chapter covers techniques to do just that.

*Chapter 7, Executable Documentation with doctest,* goes through the usage of doctest by working through one of the modules of our application.

*Chapter 8, Extending unittest with nose2,* gives us a look at nose2, a powerful test runner and plugin suite that extends the unittest framework.

*Chapter 9, Unit Testing Patterns,* covers some other patterns for unit testing. We see how to speed up tests and how we can run specific subsets of tests. We also take a look at data-driven tests and mocking patterns.

*Chapter 10, Tools to Improve Test-Driven Development,* explains some popular third-party tools to help us improve our TDD practice. Some of these tools, such as py.test and trial, are test runners with some unique features.

*Appendix A, Answers to Exercises,* contains the answers to the exercises presented throughout this book. There are many possible solutions, each with their own advantages and disadvantages.

*Appendix B, Working with Older Python Versions,* describes the changes needed in order to apply the techniques in this book for older versions of Python because this book has been written for Python 3.4.

# What you need for this book

You'll need the following software for this book: Python 3.4, nose 2, and lettuce.

# Who this book is for

This book is intended for Python developers who want to use the principles of Test-Driven Development (TDD) to create efficient and robust applications. In order to get the best out of this book, you should have development experience with Python.

# Conventions

In this book, you will find a number of text styles that distinguish between different kinds of information. Here are some examples of these styles and an explanation of their meaning.

Code words in text, database table names, folder names, filenames, file extensions, pathnames, dummy URLs, user input, and Twitter handles are shown as follows: "We can include other contexts through the use of the `include` directive."

A block of code is set as follows:

```
import unittest
class StockTest(unittest.TestCase):
    def test_price_of_a_new_stock_class_should_be_None(self):
        stock = Stock("GOOG")
        self.assertIsNone(stock.price)
if __name__ == "__main__":
    unittest.main()
```

When we wish to draw your attention to a particular part of a code block, the relevant lines or items are set in bold:

```
class Stock:
    LONG_TERM_TIMESPAN = 10
    SHORT_TERM_TIMESPAN = 5
```

Any command-line input or output is written as follows:

```
python3 -m unittest discover
```

**New terms** and **important words** are shown in bold. Words that you see on the screen, for example, in menus or dialog boxes, appear in the text like this: "Select the **Publish JUnit test result report** checkbox and enter the location of the nose2 unit test XML file."

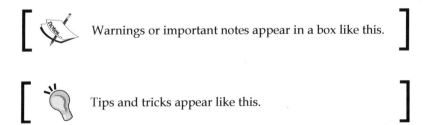

> Warnings or important notes appear in a box like this.

> Tips and tricks appear like this.

# Reader feedback

Feedback from our readers is always welcome. Let us know what you think about this book—what you liked or disliked. Reader feedback is important for us as it helps us develop titles that you will really get the most out of.

To send us general feedback, simply e-mail feedback@packtpub.com, and mention the book's title in the subject of your message.

If there is a topic that you have expertise in and you are interested in either writing or contributing to a book, see our author guide at www.packtpub.com/authors.

# Customer support

Now that you are the proud owner of a Packt book, we have a number of things to help you to get the most from your purchase.

# Downloading the example code

You can download the example code files from your account at http://www.packtpub.com for all the Packt Publishing books you have purchased. If you purchased this book elsewhere, you can visit http://www.packtpub.com/support and register to have the files e-mailed directly to you.

You can also get a copy of the code from https://github.com/siddhi/test_driven_python.

# Errata

Although we have taken every care to ensure the accuracy of our content, mistakes do happen. If you find a mistake in one of our books—maybe a mistake in the text or the code—we would be grateful if you could report this to us. By doing so, you can save other readers from frustration and help us improve subsequent versions of this book. If you find any errata, please report them by visiting http://www.packtpub.com/submit-errata, selecting your book, clicking on the **Errata Submission Form** link, and entering the details of your errata. Once your errata are verified, your submission will be accepted and the errata will be uploaded to our website or added to any list of existing errata under the Errata section of that title.

To view the previously submitted errata, go to https://www.packtpub.com/books/content/support and enter the name of the book in the search field. The required information will appear under the **Errata** section.

# Piracy

Piracy of copyrighted material on the Internet is an ongoing problem across all media. At Packt, we take the protection of our copyright and licenses very seriously. If you come across any illegal copies of our works in any form on the Internet, please provide us with the location address or website name immediately so that we can pursue a remedy.

Please contact us at copyright@packtpub.com with a link to the suspected pirated material.

We appreciate your help in protecting our authors and our ability to bring you valuable content.

# Questions

If you have a problem with any aspect of this book, you can contact us at questions@packtpub.com, and we will do our best to address the problem.

# 1
# Getting Started with Test-Driven Development

My first encounter with **Test-Driven Development** (TDD) was back in 2002. At that time, it wasn't as mainstream as it is today, and I remember watching two developers writing some tests first and then implementing the functionality later. I thought it to be quite a strange way to write a code, and I promptly forgot about it. It was not until 2004, when I was involved with a challenging project, that I remembered TDD again. We were faced with a messy code that was difficult to test and every change seemed to create a series of new bugs. I thought, why not give TDD a shot and see how it worked? Suffice to say, TDD changed my outlook on software development. We stopped writing messy spaghetti code, and started writing better designed, more maintainable code. Regression failures dropped drastically. I was hooked.

Perhaps, like me, you face some challenges in a project and want to see how TDD can help you. Or, maybe you've heard a lot of people in the industry sing the praises of TDD and you're wondering what all the fuss is about. Maybe you've been reading about how TDD will be an essential skill in the near future, and want to get up to speed on it. No matter what your motivation, I hope this book will help you reach your goal.

TDD is a lot more than just a library or an API; it is a different way of developing software. In this book, we'll discuss how to apply this process to writing Python software. We're in luck, because Python has fantastic support for TDD right out of the box. In fact, unit testing has been an integral part of the Python standard library from the Python 2.1 release back in April 2001. Numerous improvements have been added since then, and the latest version that ships with Python 3.4 has a ton of exciting features that we'll explore over the course of this book.

# Prerequisites

We will be using Python 3.4 in this book. Most of the techniques will work on Python 2.6+ as well, but some small changes may be required to the examples presented in this book in order to make them run. The *Appendix B, Working with Older Python Versions* lists these changes.

This book assumes that the reader has an intermediate level of Python understanding. In this book, we will be using Python language features such as lambdas, decorators, generators, and properties, and we assume that the reader is familiar with them. While we will give a brief description of these features as we encounter them, this book will not go into a lot of details about how they work, choosing instead to focus on how to test such code.

> Note that if you have only Python 2.x installed on your system, then go to `http://python.org` and download the latest release in the Python 3.4 series. For Linux users, if Python 3.4 is not installed on your system, then check your distribution's package repository to get the latest version. If no package exists, or you are using a non-standard or older version of a distribution, then you might have to compile it from source. The instructions to do so are available at `https://docs.python.org/devguide/setup.html`.

Since TDD is a hands-on coding activity, this book will use a lot of code snippets throughout. We recommend that you follow along by typing the code and running it yourself. It is much easier to understand the code and concepts when you can see it working (or not working) in front of you, rather than just reading through the code in this book.

> **Getting the code**
>
> You can download the example code files from your account at `http://www.packtpub.com` for all the Packt Publishing books you have purchased. If you purchased this book elsewhere, you can visit `http://www.packtpub.com/support` and register to have the files e-mailed directly to you.
>
> All the code in this book can be found online at `https://github.com/siddhi/test_driven_python`. You can select a specific branch of the repository to get the code for the start of this chapter, and work through this chapter from that starting point. You can also select a tag on the branch to get the code for the endpoint of this chapter, if you would prefer to jump to the end of the code.

# Understanding test-driven development

After all the hype in the previous paragraphs, you might be wondering what exactly test-driven development is all about, and whether it is some complex procedure that requires a lot of skill to implement. Actually, test-driven development is very simple. The flowchart below shows the three steps in the process.

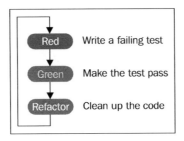

Let's walk through the preceding flowchart in a little more detail.

- **Red**: The first step is to write a small unit test case. As we have only written the test and haven't written the implementation yet, this test will naturally fail.

- **Green**: Next, we write the code that implements the desired functionality. At this point, we aren't looking to create the best design or the most readable code. We just want something simple that will pass the test.

- **Refactor**: Now that the test is passing, we go back and look at the code to see whether it can be improved. This may involve improving the design, or making it more readable or maintainable. We can use the tests written so far to ensure that we aren't breaking anything during the refactoring step.

- The cycle repeats as we proceed to the next test and implement the next bit of functionality.

Developers who are familiar with TDD usually go through this cycle many times an hour, implementing small steps of functionality each time.

# TDD versus unit testing versus integration testing

Before we go further, let's take a short detour to define some terms and understand the differences between them. It is very easy to get confused between these terms, and they are often used with different meanings in different places.

In the broadest sense of the term, **unit testing** simply means testing a single unit of code, isolated from other code that it might be integrated with. Traditionally, unit testing was an activity that was primarily performed by test engineers. These engineers would take code given by the developers and run them through a suite of tests to verify that the code worked. Since this code was tested before integration, the process fits into the definition of a unit test. Traditional unit testing was typically a manual affair, with test engineers walking through the tests cases by hand, although some teams would go a step further and automate the tests.

An **integration test** is a test that involves exercising more than one unit of the system. The goal is to check whether these units have been integrated correctly. A typical integration test might be to go to a web page, fill in a form, and check whether the right message is displayed on the screen. In order for this test to pass, the UI must show the form correctly, the input must be captured correctly, and that input must be passed on to any logic processing. The steps might involve reading and writing from a database before a message is generated and the UI has to display it correctly. Only if all these interactions succeed will the integration test pass. If any one step should fail, the integration test will fail.

At this point, a valid question would be to ask why we need unit testing at all. Why not write only integration tests, where a single test could check so many parts of the application at once? The reason is that integration tests do not pinpoint the location of failure. A failing integration test could have an error in the UI, or in the logic, or somewhere in the way data is read or written. It will take a lot of investigation to see where the error is and fix it. By contrast, with well-written unit tests, a failing unit test will pinpoint exactly what is failing. Developers can go right to the point and fix the error.

Along the way, teams started moving to a process where developers themselves wrote tests for the code that they had implemented. These tests would be written after the developer had finished the implementation, and helped verify that the code worked as expected. These tests were usually automated. Such a process is generally called **developer testing** or **developer unit testing**.

TDD takes developer tests one step further, by writing the test before starting the implementation.

- **Developer tests**: Any kind of automated unit tests written by the developer, either before or after functionality is implemented.

- **Unit testing**: Any kind of testing of a particular unit of an application, either by a developer or a tester. These tests might be automated, or run manually.

- **Integration testing**: Any kind of testing that involves two or more units working together. These tests are typically performed by a tester, but they could be done by a developer as well. These tests might be manual or automated.

As we can see, unit testing is a general term, whereas developer testing is a specific subset of unit testing, and TDD is a specific form of developer testing.

On the surface, traditional unit testing, developer testing and TDD look similar. They all appear to be about writing tests for a single unit of code, with only minor variations based on who writes the test and whether the tests are written before the code or after.

However, dig deeper and differences appear. First, the intent is vastly different. Traditional unit testing and developer testing are all about writing tests to verify that the code works as it is supposed to. On the other hand, the main focus of TDD is not really about testing. The simple act of writing a test before the implementation changes the way we think when we implement the corresponding functionality. The resulting code is more testable, usually has a simple and elegant design, and is more maintainable and readable. This is because making a class easy to test also encourages good design practices, such as decoupling dependencies and writing small, modular classes.

Thus, one can say that TDD is all about writing better code, and it is just a happy side effect that we end up with a fully automated test suite as an outcome.

This difference in intent manifests itself in the type of tests. Developer testing usually results in large test cases, with a hefty part of the test code involved in test setup. By contrast, tests written using TDD are very small and numerous. Some people like to call them micro tests to differentiate them from other developer tests or traditional unit tests. TDD-style unit tests also try to be very fast to run because they are executed every few minutes during the development process.

Finally, the tests that are written in TDD are those that drive the development forward, and not necessarily those that cover all imaginable scenarios. For example, a function that is supposed to process a file might have tests to handle cases when the file exists or it doesn't exist, but probably won't have tests to see what happens if the file is 1 terabyte in size. The latter is something that a tester might conceivably test for, but would be an unusual test in TDD unless the function is clearly expected to work with such a file.

This really highlights the difference between TDD and other forms of unit testing.

 TDD is about writing better, cleaner, more maintainable code, and only incidentally about testing.

# Using TDD to build a stock alert application

Over the course of this book, we are going to be using TDD to build a simple stock alert application. The application will listen to stock updates from a source. The source can be anything—a server on the Internet, or a file on the hard drive, or something else. We will be able to define rules, and when the rule is matched, the application sends us an email or text message.

For example, we could define a rule as "If AAPL crosses the $550 level then send me an email". Once defined, the application will monitor updates and send an e-mail when the rule is matched.

## Writing our first test

Enough talk. Let's get started with our application. What is a good place to start? From examining the application description mentioned earlier, it looks like we will need the following modules:

- Some way to read stock price updates, either from the Internet or from a file
- A way to manage the stock information so that we can process it
- A way to define rules and match them against the current stock information
- A way to send an email or text message when a rule is matched

Based on these requirements, we will be using the following design:

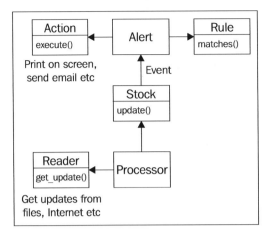

Each term is discussed as follows:

- **Alert**: This is the core of the application. An alert will take a **Rule** and map it to an **Action**. When the rule is matched, the action is executed.

- **Rule**: A **Rule** contains the condition we want to check for. We should get alerted when the rule is matched.

- **Action**: This is the action to be performed when the rule is matched. This could be as simple as printing a message on the screen, or, in more real-work scenarios, we might send an e-mail or a text message.

- **Stock**: The **Stock** class keeps track of the current price and possibly a history of the prices for a stock. It sends an **Event** to the **Alert** when there is an update. The alert then checks if it's rule matched and whether any action needs to be executed.

- **Event**: This class is used to send events to the **Alert** when a **Stock** is updated.

- **Processor**: The processor takes stock updates from the **Reader** and updates the **Stock** with the latest data. Updating the stock causes the event to be fired, which, in turn, causes the alert to check for a rule match.

- **Reader**: The **Reader** gets the stock alerts from some source. In this book, we are going to get updates from a simple list or a file, but you can build other readers to get updates from the Internet or elsewhere.

Among all these classes, the way to manage stock information seems to be the simplest, so let's start there. What we are going to do is to create a `Stock` class. This class will hold information about the current stock. It will store the current price and possibly some recent price history. We can then use this class when we want to match rules later on.

To get started, create a directory called `src`. This directory is going to hold all our source code. In the rest of this book, we will refer to this directory as the project root. Inside the `src` directory, create a subdirectory called `stock_alerter`. This is the directory in which we are going to implement our stock alert module.

Okay, let's get started with implementing the class.

NO! Wait! Remember the TDD process that was described earlier? The first step is to write a test, before we code the implementation. By writing the test first, we now have the opportunity to think about what we want this class to do.

So what exactly do we want this class to do? Let's start with something simple:

- A `Stock` class should be instantiated with the ticker symbol
- Once instantiated, and before any updates, the price should be `None`

Of course, there are many more things we will want this class to do, but we'll think about them later. Rather than coming up with a very comprehensive list of functionality, we're going to focus on tiny bits of functionality, one at a time. For now, the preceding expectation is good enough.

To convert the preceding expectation into code, create a file called `stock.py` in the project root, and put the following code in it:

```python
import unittest

class StockTest(unittest.TestCase):
    def test_price_of_a_new_stock_class_should_be_None(self):
        stock = Stock("GOOG")
        self.assertIsNone(stock.price)

if __name__ == "__main__":
    unittest.main()
```

What does this code do?

1. First, we import `unittest`. This is the library that has the test framework that we are going to use. Luckily for us, it is bundled into the Python standard library by default and is always available, so we don't need to install anything, we can just import the module directly.

2. Second, we create a class `StockTest`. This class will hold all the test cases for the `Stock` class. This is just a convenient way of grouping related tests together. There is no rule that every class should have a corresponding test class. Sometimes, if we have a lot of tests for a class, then we may want to create separate test classes for each individual behavior, or group the tests some other way. However, in most cases, creating one test class for an actual class is the best way to go about it.

3. Our `StockTest` class inherits from the `TestCase` class in the `unittest` module. All tests need to inherit from this class in order to be identified as a test class.

4. Inside the class, we have one method. This method is a test case. The `unittest` framework will pick up any method that starts with `test`. The method has a name that describes what the test is checking for. This is just so that when we come back after a few months, we still remember what the test does.

5. The test creates a `Stock` object and then checks if the price is `None`. `assertIsNone` is a method provided by the `TestCase` class that we are inheriting from. It checks that its parameter is `None`. If the parameter is not `None`, it raises an `AssertionError` and fails the test. Otherwise, execution continues to the next line. Since that is the last line of the method, the test completes and is marked as a pass.

6. The last segment checks if the module was executed directly from the command line. In such a case, the `__name__` variable will have the value `__main__`, and the code will execute the `unittest.main()` function. This function will scan the current file for all tests and execute them. The reason we need to wrap this function call inside the conditional is because this part does not get executed if the module is imported into another file.

Congratulations! You have your first failing test. Normally, a failing test would be a cause for worry, but in this case, a failing test means that we're done with the first step of the process and can move on to the next step.

# Analyzing the test output

Now that we've written our test, it is time to run it. To run the test, just execute the file. Assuming that the current directory is the `src` directory, the following is the command to execute the file:

- Windows:

  ```
  python.exe stock_alerter\stock.py
  ```

- Linux/Mac:

  ```
  python3 stock_alerter/stock.py
  ```

If the python executable is not on your path, then you will have to give the full path to the executable here. In some Linux distributions, the file may be called `python34` or `python3.4` instead of `python3`.

When we run the file, the output looks like the following:

```
E
======================================================================
ERROR: test_price_of_a_new_stock_class_should_be_None (__main__.
StockTest)
----------------------------------------------------------------------
Traceback (most recent call last):
  File "stock_alerter\stock.py", line 6, in test_price_of_a_new_stock_
class_should_be_None
    stock = Stock("GOOG")
NameError: name 'Stock' is not defined
----------------------------------------------------------------------
Ran 1 test in 0.001s


FAILED (errors=1)
```

As expected, the test fails, because we haven't created the `Stock` class yet.

Let's look at that output in a little more detail:

- `E` on the first line signifies that the test gave an error. If a test passed, then you would have a dot on that line. A failed test would be marked with `F`. Since we have only a single test, there is only one character there. When we have multiple tests, then the status of each test will be displayed on that line, one character per test.

- After all the test statuses are displayed, we get a more detailed explanation of any test errors and failures. It tells us whether there was a failure or an error (in this case denoted by ERROR) followed by the name of the test and which class it belongs to. This is followed by a traceback, so we know where the failure occurred.

- Finally, there is a summary that shows how many tests were executed, how many passed or failed, and how many gave errors.

# Test errors versus test failures

There are two reasons why a test might not pass: It might have failed or it might have caused an error. There is a small difference between these two. A **failure** indicates that we expected some outcome (usually via an assert), but got something else. For example, in our test, we are asserting that `stock.price` is `None`. Suppose `stock.price` has some other value apart from `None`, then the test will fail.

An error indicates that something unexpected happened, usually an unexpected exception was raised. In our previous example, we got an error because the `Stock` class has not yet been defined.

In both the cases, the test does not pass, but for different reasons, and these are reported separately as test failures and test errors.

# Making the test pass

Now that we have a failing test, let's make it pass. Add the following code to the `stock.py` file, after the `import unittest` line:

```
class Stock:
    def __init__(self, symbol):
        self.symbol = symbol
        self.price = None
```

What we have done here is to implement just enough code to pass the test. We've created the `Stock` class so the test shouldn't complain about it being missing, and we've initialized the `price` attribute to `None`.

What about the rest of the implementation for this class? This can wait. Our main focus right now is to pass the current expectation for this class. As we write more tests, we will end up implementing more of the class as well.

Run the file again, and this time the output should be like the following:

```
.
----------------------------------------------------------------
Ran 1 test in 0.000s

OK
```

We've got a dot in the first line, which signifies that the test is passing. The OK message at the end tells us that all tests have passed.

The final step is to refactor the code. With so little code, there is really nothing much to clean up. So, we can skip the refactoring step and start with the next test.

# Reorganizing the test code

We've added the test cases in the same file as the code. This is a good, simple way to add test cases to standalone scripts and applications that are not too complex. However, for larger applications, it is a good idea to keep test code separate from production code.

There are two common patterns for organizing test code this way.

The first pattern is to keep test code in a separate root directory, as shown in the following:

```
root
|
+- package
|  |
|  +- file1
|  +- file2
|
+- test
   |
   +- test_file1
   +- test_file2
```

The other pattern is to keep test code as a submodule of the main code, as shown in the following:

```
root
|
+- package
   |
   +- file1
   +- file2
   +- test
      |
      +- test_file1
      +- test_file2
```

The first pattern is commonly used for standalone modules as it allows us to distribute the code and tests together. Tests can generally be run without having to perform a lot of setup or configuration. The second pattern has an advantage when the application has to be packaged without the test code, for example when deploying to production servers, or distributing to customers (in the case of a commercial application). However, both the patterns are in popular use, and it is mainly a personal preference as to which method to use.

We are going to follow the first pattern in this book. To get started, create a directory called tests inside the stock_alerter directory. Next, create a file called test_stock.py in this directory. We will put all our test cases in one-to-one correspondence with the source file. This means, a file called sample.py will have its test cases in the tests/test_sample.py file. This is a simple naming convention that helps to quickly locate test cases.

Finally, we move our test cases into this file. We also need to import the Stock class to be able to use it in the test case. Our test_stock.py file now looks like the following:

```python
import unittest
from ..stock import Stock


class StockTest(unittest.TestCase):
    def test_price_of_a_new_stock_class_should_be_None(self):
        stock = Stock("GOOG")
        self.assertIsNone(stock.price)
```

Remember to remove the `import unittest` line from `stock.py`, now that it no longer contains the test code. Previously we had just one standalone script, but we now have a `stock_alerter` module and a `stock_alerter.tests` submodule. Since we are now working with modules, we should also add in an empty `__init__.py` file in both the `stock_alerter` and `tests` directories.

Our file layout should now be like the following:

```
src
|
+- stock_alerter
   |
   +- __init__.py
   +- stock.py
   +- tests
      +- __init__.py
      +- test_stock.py
```

# Running the tests after the reorganization

If you have noticed, we no longer have a call to `unittest.main()` in the test code. Including a call to `unittest.main()` works well with individual scripts since it allows us to run the tests by simply executing the file. However, it is not a very scalable solution. If we have hundreds of files, we would like to run all the tests at once, and not have to execute each file individually.

To address this, Python 3 comes with a very nice test discovery and execution capability from the command line. Simply go into the `src` directory and run the following command:

- Windows:

  ```
  python.exe -m unittest
  ```

- Linux/Mac:

  ```
  python3 -m unittest
  ```

This command will go through the current directory and all subdirectories and run all the tests that are found. This is the default autodiscover mode of execution, where the command searches all the files and runs the tests. Autodiscovery can also be explicitly run with the following command:

```
python3 -m unittest discover
```

Autodiscover can be customized to check in specific directories or files with the following parameters:

- `-s start_directory`: Specify the start directory from where the discovery should start. This defaults to the current directory.

- `-t top_directory`: Specify the top-level directory. This is the directory from which imports are performed. This is important if the start directory is inside the package and you get errors due to incorrect imports. This defaults to the start directory.

- `-p file_pattern`: The file pattern that identifies test files. By default it checks for python files that start with `test`. If we name our test files something else (for example, `stock_test.py`), then we have to pass in this parameter so that the file is correctly identified as a test file.

To illustrate the difference between the start and top directory, run the following command from the `src` directory:

```
python3 -m unittest discover -s stock_alerter
```

The preceding command will fail with an import error. The reason is because when the start directory is set to `stock_alerter`, then the `tests` directory is imported as a top-level module, and the relative import fails. To get around this, we need to use the following command:

```
python3 -m unittest discover -s stock_alerter -t .
```

This command will import all modules relative to the top directory, and so `stock_alerter` correctly becomes the main module.

You can also disable autodiscovery and specify only certain tests to be run:

- Passing in a module name will only run the tests within that module. For example, `python3 -m unittest stock_alerter.tests.test_stock` will run the tests only in `test_stock.py`.

- You can further refine to a specific class or method, such as `python3 -m unittest stock_alerter.tests.test_stock.StockTest`.

# Summary

Congratulations! You've completed one cycle of TDD. As you can see, each cycle is very quick. Some cycles, like the one we've just gone through, can be completed in a few seconds. Other cycles might involve a fair amount of cleanup and can take quite a long time. Each cycle will implement a small test, a small bit of functionality to pass the test, and then some cleanup to make the code of high quality.

In this chapter, we looked at what TDD is, how it is different from other forms of unit and integration testing, and wrote our first test.

At this point, our implementation is still very small and very simple. You might be wondering if it is worth all this hype just to write and implement four lines of very simple code. In the next few chapters, we'll progress further with the examples and go more in-depth into the process.

# 2
# Red-Green-Refactor – The TDD Cycle

In the previous chapter, we went through a small TDD cycle by creating a failing test and then making it pass. In this chapter, we are going to fill out the rest of the Stock class by writing more tests. In the process, we will dig deeper into the TDD cycle and the unittest module.

## Tests are executable requirements

In the first test, we wrote a very simple test that checked whether a new Stock class has its price attribute initialized to None. We can now think about what requirement we want to implement next.

An observant reader might have caught on to the terminology used in the previous sentence, where I said that we can think about the requirement to implement next, instead of saying that we can think about the test to write next. Both statements are equivalent, because in TDD, tests are nothing but requirements. Each time we write a test and implement code to make it pass, what we actually do is make the code meet some requirement. Looking at it another way, tests are just executable requirement specifications. Requirement documentation often goes out of sync with what is actually implemented, but this is impossible with tests, because the moment they go out of sync, the test will fail.

In the previous chapter, we said that the `Stock` class will be used to hold price information and price history for a stock symbol. This suggests that we need a way to set the price whenever it is updated. Let us implement an `update` method that meets the following requirements:

- It should take a timestamp and price value and set it on the object
- The price cannot be negative
- After multiple updates, the object gives us the latest price

# Arrange-Act-Assert

Let us start with the first requirement. Here is the test:

```
def test_stock_update(self):
    """An update should set the price on the stock object
    We will be using the `datetime` module for the timestamp
    """
    goog = Stock("GOOG")
    goog.update(datetime(2014, 2, 12), price=10)
    self.assertEqual(10, goog.price)
```

Here we call the `update` method (which doesn't exist yet) with the timestamp and price and then check that the price has been set correctly. We use the `assertEqual` method provided in the `unittest.TestCase` class to assert the value.

Since we are using the `datetime` module to set the timestamp, we will have to add the line `from datetime import datetime` to the top of the file before it will run.

This test follows the pattern of Arrange-Act-Assert.

1. **Arrange**: Set up the context for the test. In this case, we create a `Stock` object. In other tests, it may involve creating multiple objects or hooking a few things together that will be required by the particular test.
2. **Act**: Perform the action that we want to test. Here, we call the `update` method with the appropriate arguments.
3. **Assert**: Finally we assert that the outcome was as expected.

In this test, each part of the pattern took one line of code, but this is not always the case. Often there will be more than one line for each part of the test.

# Documenting our tests

When we run the tests, we get the following output:

```
.E
================================================================
ERROR: test_stock_update (__main__.StockTest)
An update should set the price on the stock object
----------------------------------------------------------------
Traceback (most recent call last):
  File "stock_alerter\stock.py", line 22, in test_stock_update
    goog.update(datetime(2014, 2, 12), price=10)
AttributeError: 'Stock' object has no attribute 'update'


----------------------------------------------------------------
Ran 2 tests in 0.001s
FAILED (errors=1)
```

The test fails as expected, but the interesting thing is that the first line of the docstring is printed out on the fourth line. This is useful because we get some more information on which case is failing. This shows a second way of documenting out tests by using the first line for a short summary, and the rest of the docstring for a more detailed explanation. The detailed explanation will not be printed out with a test failure, so there is no problem with cluttering the test failure output.

We have used two ways of documenting tests:

- Writing a descriptive test method name
- Putting an explanation in the docstring

Which is better? Most of the time the test is self explanatory and doesn't need a whole lot of background explanation. In such cases, a well named test method is sufficient.

However, sometimes the test method name becomes so long that it becomes clumsy and actually ends up reducing the readability of the code. At other times, we might want to put in a more detailed explanation of what we are testing and why. In such cases, shortening the method name and putting the explanation in the docstring is a good idea.

Here is the implementation to make this test pass:

```
def update(self, timestamp, price):
    self.price = price
```

This minimal implementation passes the test. As with the first bit of implementation, we aren't trying to implement the whole functionality. We want to implement just enough to make the test pass. Remember, when the test passes, it means the requirement is met. At this point, we have two passing tests, and we don't really have anything to refactor, so let us move on.

# Testing for exceptions

Another requirement is that the price should not be negative. We would want to raise a `ValueError` if the price is negative. How would we check for this expectation in a test? Here is one way to do that:

```
def test_negative_price_should_throw_ValueError(self):
    goog = Stock("GOOG")
    try:
        goog.update(datetime(2014, 2, 13), -1)
    except ValueError:
        return
    self.fail("ValueError was not raised")
```

In the preceding code, we call the `update` method with a negative price. This call is wrapped with a `try...except` block to catch `ValueError`. If the exception is raised correctly, then control goes into the `except` block where we return from the test. Since the test method returned successfully, it is marked as passing. If the exception is not raised, then the `fail` method gets called. This is another method provided by `unittest.TestCase` and raises a test failure exception when it is called. We can pass in a message to provide some explanation as to why it failed.

Here is the code to pass this test:

```
def update(self, timestamp, price):
    if price < 0:
        raise ValueError("price should not be negative")
    self.price = price
```

With this code, all the three tests so far pass.

Since checking for exceptions is quite a common case, `unittest` provides a simpler way to do it:

```
def test_negative_price_should_throw_ValueError(self):
    goog = Stock("GOOG")
    self.assertRaises(ValueError, goog.update,
        datetime(2014, 2, 13), -1)
```

The `assertRaises` method takes the expected exception as the first argument, the function to call as the second argument, and the parameters to the function are passed as in the remaining arguments. If you need to call the function with keyword arguments, then they can be passed in as keyword arguments to the `assertRaises` method.

 Note that the second argument to `assertRaises` is a reference to the function to be called. This is why we don't put parentheses after the function name.

If passing in a function reference and a list of parameters feels awkward, then `assertRaises` provides another syntax that we can use:

```
def test_negative_price_should_throw_ValueError(self):
    goog = Stock("GOOG")
    with self.assertRaises(ValueError):
        goog.update(datetime(2014, 2, 13), -1)
```

What is going on here? When we pass only one parameter to `assertRaises`, a context manager is returned. We can use that with the `with` statement and put our action in that block. If the block raises the expected exception, then the context manager matches it and exits the block without an error. However, if the expected exception is not raised in the block, then the context manager raises a failure when the block is exited.

# Exploring assert methods

Now we have just one requirement for `update` remaining:

- **-Done-** It should take a timestamp and price value and set it on the object
- **-Done-** The price cannot be negative
- After multiple updates, the object gives us the latest price

Let us take the remaining requirement. Here is the test:

```
def test_stock_price_should_give_the_latest_price(self):
    goog = Stock("GOOG")
    goog.update(datetime(2014, 2, 12), price=10)
    goog.update(datetime(2014, 2, 13), price=8.4)
    self.assertAlmostEqual(8.4, goog.price, delta=0.0001)
```

What this test does is to simply call `update` twice, and when we ask for the price, provide us with the newer one. The interesting point about the test is that we use the `assertAlmostEqual` method here. This method is often used when checking equality with floating point numbers. Why don't we use plain old `assertEqual`? The reason is that due to the way floating points are stored, the result may not be exactly the number you expect. There could be a very small difference between what you expect and the actual number that is stored. Taking this into account, the `assertAlmostEqual` method allows us to specify a tolerance in the comparison. So, for example, if we expect 8.4 but the actual value is 8.39999999, the test will still pass.

The `assertAlmostEqual` method has two ways of specifying tolerance. The method we used above involves passing in a `delta` parameter which says that the difference between the expected value and the actual value should be within the delta. We've specified the `delta` parameter above as `0.0001`, which means any value between 8.3999 and 8.4001 will pass the test.

The other way of specifying tolerance is to use the `places` parameter as shown in the following code:

```
self.assertAlmostEqual(8.4, goog.price, places=4)
```

If this parameter is used, then both the expected and the actual values are rounded to the given number of decimal places before being compared. Note that you need to pass either the `delta` parameter or the `places` parameter. It is an error to pass both parameters together.

So far, we've used the following assertion methods:

- `assertIsNone`
- `assertEqual`
- `assertRaises`
- `assertAlmostEqual`
- `fail`

The `unittest` module provides a large number of assertion methods that we can use for various conditions. Some of the common ones are listed below:

- `assertFalse(x, msg)`, `assertTrue(x, msg)`
- `assertIsNone(x, msg)`, `assertIsNotNone(x, msg)`
- `assertEqual(x, y, msg)`, `assertNotEqual(x, y, msg)`
- `assertAlmostEqual(x, y, places, msg, delta)`, `assertNotAlmostEqual(x, y, places, msg, delta)`
- `assertGreater(x, y, msg)`, `assertGreaterEqual(x, y, msg)`
- `assertLess(x, y, msg)`, `assertLessEqual(x, y, msg)`
- `assertIs(x, y, msg)`, `assertIsNot(x, y, msg)`
- `assertIn(x, seq, msg)`, `assertNotIn(x, seq, msg)`
- `assertIsInstance(x, cls, msg)`, `assertNotIsInstance(x, cls, msg)`
- `assertRegex(text, regex, msg)`, `assertNotRegex(text, regex, msg)`
- `assertRaises(exception, callable, *args, **kwargs)`
- `fail(msg)`

Most of the preceding functions are self explanatory. The following are some points that require a bit of explanation:

- `msg` parameter: Most of the assert methods take an optional message parameter. A string can be passed here and it will be printed out in case the assertion fails. Usually, the default message is quite descriptive and this parameter is not required. Most of the time it is used with the `fail` method, as we saw a little while ago.

- `assertEqual` versus `assertIs`: These two sets of assertions are very similar. The critical difference is that the former checks for *equality* while the latter assertion is used to check for object *identity*. The second assertion fails in previous example because although both objects are equal, they are still two different objects, and hence their identity is different:

```
>>> test = unittest.TestCase()
>>> test.assertEqual([1, 2], [1, 2])   # Assertion Passes
>>> test.assertIs([1, 2], [1, 2])      # Assertion Fails
Traceback (most recent call last):
  File "<stdin>", line 1, in <module>
  File "C:\Python34\lib\unittest\case.py", line 1067, in assertIs
    self.fail(self._formatMessage(msg, standardMsg))
```

```
File "C:\Python34\lib\unittest\case.py", line 639, in fail
    raise self.failureException(msg)
AssertionError: [1, 2] is not [1, 2]
```

- `assertIn`/`assertNotIn`: These asserts are used to check if an element is present in a sequence. This includes strings, lists, sets, and any other object that supports the `in` operator.

- `assertIsInstance`/`assertNotIsInstance`: They check if an object is an instance of the given class. The `cls` parameter can also be a tuple of classes, to assert that the object is an instance of any one of them.

The `unittest` module also provides some less-frequently-used assertions:

- `assertRaisesRegex(exception, regex, callable, *args, **kwargs)`: This assertion is similar to `assertRaises`, except that it takes an additional `regex` parameter. A regular expression can be passed in here and the assertion will check that the right exception was raised, as well as that the exception message matches the regular expression.

- `assertWarns(warning, callable, *args, **kwargs)`: It is similar to `assertRaises`, but checks that a warning was raised instead.

- `assertWarnsRegex(warning, callable, *args, **kwargs)`: It is the warning equivalent of `assertRaisesRegex`.

# Specific asserts versus generic asserts

One question that might come to your mind is why there are so many different assert methods. Why can't we just use `assertTrue` instead of the more specific assert, as shown in the following code:

```
assertInSeq(x, seq)
assertTrue(x in seq)


assertEqual(10, x)
assertTrue(x == 10)
```

While they are certainly equivalent, one motivation for using a specific assert is that you get a better error message if the assertion fails. When comparing objects like lists and dicts, the error message will show exactly where the difference occurs, making it much easier to understand. Therefore, it is recommended to use the more specific asserts wherever possible.

# Setup and teardown

Let us take a look at the tests that we have done so far:

```python
def test_price_of_a_new_stock_class_should_be_None(self):
    stock = Stock("GOOG")
    self.assertIsNone(stock.price)


def test_stock_update(self):
    """An update should set the price on the stock object
    We will be using the `datetime` module for the timestamp
    """
    goog = Stock("GOOG")
    goog.update(datetime(2014, 2, 12), price=10)
    self.assertEqual(10, goog.price)


def test_negative_price_should_throw_ValueError(self):
    goog = Stock("GOOG")
    with self.assertRaises(ValueError):
        goog.update(datetime(2014, 2, 13), -1)


def test_stock_price_should_give_the_latest_price(self):
    goog = Stock("GOOG")
    goog.update(datetime(2014, 2, 12), price=10)
    goog.update(datetime(2014, 2, 13), price=8.4)
    self.assertAlmostEqual(8.4, goog.price, delta=0.0001)
```

If you notice, each test does the same setup by instantiating a `Stock` object that is then used in the test. In this case, the setup is just one line, but sometimes we might have to do multiple steps before we are ready to run the test. Instead of repeating this setup code in each and every test, we can make use of the `setUp` method provided by the `TestCase` class:

```python
def setUp(self):
    self.goog = Stock("GOOG")


def test_price_of_a_new_stock_class_should_be_None(self):
    self.assertIsNone(self.goog.price)


def test_stock_update(self):
```

```
        """An update should set the price on the stock object
        We will be  using the `datetime` module for the timestamp
        """
        self.goog.update(datetime(2014, 2, 12), price=10)
        self.assertEqual(10, self.goog.price)


    def test_negative_price_should_throw_ValueError(self):
        with self.assertRaises(ValueError):
            self.goog.update(datetime(2014, 2, 13), -1)


    def test_stock_price_should_give_the_latest_price(self):
        self.goog.update(datetime(2014, 2, 12), price=10)
        self.goog.update(datetime(2014, 2, 13), price=8.4)
        self.assertAlmostEqual(8.4, self.goog.price, delta=0.0001)
```

In the preceding code, we are overriding the default `setUp` method with our own. We've put our setup code in this method. This method is executed before every test, so the initialization done here is available for our test method to use. Note that we have to change our tests to use `self.goog` since it has now become an instance variable.

Similar to `setUp`, a `tearDown` method is also available which is executed immediately after the test is executed. We can do any required cleanup in this method.

The `setUp` and `tearDown` methods are executed before and after every test. What if we want some setup to be done only once for a group of tests? The `setupUpClass` and `tearDownClass` methods can be implemented as class methods and will be executed only once per test class. Similarly, the `setupUpModule` and `tearDownModule` functions are available to do any initialization once for the whole module. The following example shows the order of execution:

```
import unittest


def setUpModule():
    print("setUpModule")


def tearDownModule():
    print("tearDownModule")


class Class1Test(unittest.TestCase):
    @classmethod
```

```
    def setUpClass(cls):
        print("  setUpClass")


    @classmethod
    def tearDownClass(cls):
        print("  tearDownClass")


    def setUp(self):
        print("        setUp")


    def tearDown(self):
        print("        tearDown")


    def test_1(self):
        print("          class 1 test 1")


    def test_2(self):
        print("          class 1 test 2")

class Class2Test(unittest.TestCase):
    def test_1(self):
        print("          class 2 test 1")
```

When this code is run, the output is as follows:

```
setUpModule
  setUpClass
        setUp
          class 1 test 1
        tearDown
        setUp
          class 1 test 2
        tearDown
  tearDownClass
          class 2 test 1
tearDownModule
```

As we can see, the module level setup is executed first, followed by the class level, and finally the test case level. The teardown is executed in reverse order. In practical use, the test case level `setUp` and `tearDown` methods are very commonly used, while class level and module level setups are not needed much. Class level and module level setups are only used when there is an expensive setup step, such as making a connection to a database or a remote server, and it is preferable to do this setup just once and share it between all the tests.

**A warning when using class level and module level setup**

Any initialization done at class and module levels is shared between tests. Hence, it is important that modifications made in one test do not affect the other. For example, if we had initialized `self.goog = Stock("GOOG")` in `setUpClass`, it could have led to an unexpected failure, since the first test to check that the price of a new `Stock` object should be `None` will fail if one of the other tests is executed before it and it changes the state of the object.

Remember that the order in which tests are run is not guaranteed. Tests should be independent and should pass no matter the order they are executed in. Therefore, it is crucial that `setUpClass` and `setUpModule` are used carefully to only setup state which can be reused between tests.

# Brittle tests

We've implemented the three requirements for the `update` method:

- **-Done-** It should take a timestamp and price value and set it on the object
- **-Done-** After multiple updates, the object gives us the latest price
- **-Done-** The price cannot be negative

Now, let us suppose that a new requirement comes up that we had not known about before:

- The `Stock` class needs a method to check if the stock has an increasing trend. An increasing trend is one where each of the latest three updates is an increase over the previous one.

So far, our `Stock` implementation just stores the latest price. In order to implement this functionality, we need to store some history of past price values. One way to do this is to change the `price` variable to a list. The problem is that when we change the internals of our implementation, it would break all of our tests, because all of them access the `price` variable directly and assert that it has specific values.

What we see here is an example of test brittleness.

A test is brittle when a change in the implementation details requires a change in the test cases. Ideally, a test should be testing the interface and not the implementation directly. After all, it is the interface that other units will be using to interact with this unit. When we test through the interface, it allows us the freedom to change the implementation of code without worrying about breaking the tests.

**There are three ways a test might fail:**
- If there is a bug introduced in the code being tested
- If the test is tightly coupled to an implementation and we make changes to the code that modify the implementation, but without introducing a bug (for example, renaming a variable or modifying the internal design)
- If the test requires some resource that is unavailable (for example, connecting to an external server, but the server is down)

Ideally, the first case should be the only case where a test should fail. We should try to avoid the second and third as much as possible.

Sometimes it might be important to test specific implementation details. For example, suppose we have a class that is expected to perform a complex calculation and cache it for future use. The only way to test the caching functionality would be to verify if the calculated value is stored in the cache. If we later change the caching method (for example, moving from a file cache to memcache), then we will have to change the test as well.

Brittle tests can be worse than no tests, as the maintenance overhead of having to fix ten or twenty tests with every change in the implementation can turn developers away from TDD, increase the amount of frustration, and lead to teams disabling or skipping testing. Here are some guidelines on how to think about test brittleness:

- If at all possible, avoid using implementation details in tests, and only use the publicly exposed interface. This includes using only the interface methods in setup code and assertions.

- If the test needs to check functionality that is internal to the unit being tested, and it is an important functionality, then it might make sense to check for specific implementation actions.

- If it is cumbersome to use the external interface to set up the exact state that we want, or there is no interface method that retrieves the specific value we want to assert, then we may need to peek into the implementation in our tests.

- If we are fairly confident that the implementation details are very unlikely to change in the future, then we might go ahead and use implementation-specific details in the test.

For the second and third cases, the important point is to understand that there is a tradeoff between convenience, test readability, and brittleness. There is no right answer and it is a subjective decision that needs to be taken, weighing up the pros and cons of each specific situation.

# Refactoring the design

In the previous section, we talked about the new requirement of having to check if a stock has an increasing trend.

Let us start by writing a test first:

```
class StockTrendTest(unittest.TestCase):
    def setUp(self):
        self.goog = Stock("GOOG")

    def test_increasing_trend_is_true_
        if_price_increase_for_3_updates(self):
        timestamps = [datetime(2014, 2, 11), datetime(2014, 2,
            12), datetime(2014, 2, 13)]
        prices = [8, 10, 12]
        for timestamp, price in zip(timestamps, prices):
            self.goog.update(timestamp, price)
        self.assertTrue(self.goog.is_increasing_trend())
```

The test takes three timestamps and prices and performs an update for each one. Since all three prices are increasing, the `is_increasing_trend` method should return `True`.

To make this test pass, we need to first add support for storing price history.

In the initializer, let us replace the `price` attribute with a `price_history` list. This list will store the history of price updates, with each new update added to the end of the list:

```
    def __init__(self, symbol):
        self.symbol = symbol
        self.price_history = []
```

After making this change, all the tests will now fail, including the ones that were passing before. Only after we complete a few steps will we be able to have the tests pass again. When tests are passing, we can constantly run the tests to make sure we aren't breaking any functionality with our changes. When tests are failing, we do not have this safety net. It is inevitable that certain design changes, like the one we are making now, will temporarily make a number of tests fail until we finish the sequence of changes. We should try and minimize the time we spend making changes during failing tests, by making small changes at a time. This allows us to validate our changes as we go along.

We can now change the `update` method to store the new price in this list.

```
def update(self, timestamp, price):
    if price < 0:
        raise ValueError("price should not be negative")
    self.price_history.append(price)
```

We shall retain the current interface for getting the latest price by accessing the `price` attribute. However, since we have replaced the `price` attribute with the `price_history` list, we need to create a property that will mimic the existing interface:

```
@property
def price(self):
    return self.price_history[-1] \
        if self.price_history else None
```

With this change, we can run the tests again and see that all our previous tests are still passing, with only the new test for the trend functionality failing.

The new design now allows us to implement the code to pass the trend test:

```
def is_increasing_trend(self):
    return self.price_history[-3] < \
        self.price_history[-2] < self.price_history[-1]
```

The implementation of the method simply checks whether the last three price updates are increasing. With that code implemented, all our tests, including the new one, will pass.

**A quick primer on properties**

Properties are a feature of Python where we can delegate attribute access to a function. Since we declared price as a property, accessing Stock.price will cause the method to be called instead of searching for the attribute. In our implementation, it allows us to create an interface so that other modules can refer to the stock price as an attribute, even though there is no such actual attribute in the object.

# Refactoring tests

With the first test passing, we can go ahead with the second test:

```python
def test_increasing_trend_is_false_if_price_decreases(self):
    timestamps = [datetime(2014, 2, 11), datetime(2014, 2, 12), \
        datetime(2014, 2, 13)]
    prices = [8, 12, 10]
    for timestamp, price in zip(timestamps, prices):
        self.goog.update(timestamp, price)
    self.assertFalse(self.goog.is_increasing_trend())
```

Our implementation already passes this test, so let us move on to the third test:

```python
def test_increasing_trend_is_false_if_price_equal(self):
    timestamps = [datetime(2014, 2, 11), datetime(2014, 2, 12), \
        datetime(2014, 2, 13)]
    prices = [8, 10, 10]
    for timestamp, price in zip(timestamps, prices):
        self.goog.update(timestamp, price)
    self.assertFalse(self.goog.is_increasing_trend())
```

The current code passes this test as well. But let us pause at this point. If we look at the test cases so far, we can see that a lot of code is being repeated between tests. The setup code is also not very readable. The most important line here is the list of prices, which is getting hidden in the clutter. We need to clean this up. What we are going to do is to take the common code and put it into a helper method:

```python
class StockTrendTest(unittest.TestCase):
    def setUp(self):
```

```
        self.goog = Stock("GOOG")


    def given_a_series_of_prices(self, prices):
        timestamps = [datetime(2014, 2, 10), datetime(2014, 2, \
            11), datetime(2014, 2, 12), datetime(2014, 2, 13)]
        for timestamp, price in zip(timestamps, prices):
            self.goog.update(timestamp, price)


    def test_increasing_trend_is_true_
        if_price_increase_for_3_updates(self):
        self.given_a_series_of_prices([8, 10, 12])
        self.assertTrue(self.goog.is_increasing_trend())


    def test_increasing_trend_is_false_if_price_decreases(self):
        self.given_a_series_of_prices([8, 12, 10])
        self.assertFalse(self.goog.is_increasing_trend())


    def test_increasing_trend_is_false_if_price_equal(self):
        self.given_a_series_of_prices([8, 10, 10])
        self.assertFalse(self.goog.is_increasing_trend())
```

Much better! Not only is the duplication removed, but the tests are a lot more readable. By default, the `unittest` module looks for methods that start with the word `test` and only executes those methods as tests, so there is no risk that our helper method will be mistaken for a test case.

 Remember that test cases are also code. All the rules of writing clean, maintainable, and readable code apply to the test cases as well.

# Exploring the Rule classes

So far we have concentrated on the `Stock` class. Let us now turn our attention to the rule classes.

 From this point in the book, we will look at the implementation code, and then show how we can test it effectively. Note, however, that this does not mean writing the code first, followed by the unit test. The TDD process is still test first, followed by the implementation. It is the test case which will drive the implementation strategy. We are showing the implementation code first, only because it makes it easier to understand the testing concepts that will follow. All this code was originally written test first!

The rule classes keep track of the rules that the user wants to track and they can be of different types. For example, send an alert when a stock crosses a value, or matches a trend.

Here is an example of a `PriceRule` implementation:

```
class PriceRule:
    """PriceRule is a rule that triggers when a stock price
    satisfies a condition (usually greater, equal or lesser
    than a given value)"""

    def __init__(self, symbol, condition):
        self.symbol = symbol
        self.condition = condition

    def matches(self, exchange):
        try:
            stock = exchange[self.symbol]
        except KeyError:
            return False
        return self.condition(stock) if stock.price else False

    def depends_on(self):
        return {self.symbol}
```

This class is initialized with a stock symbol and a condition. The condition can be a lambda or a function that takes a stock as a parameter and returns `True` or `False`. The rule matches when the stock matches the condition. The key method for this is the `matches` method. This method returns `True` or `False` depending on whether the rule is matched or not. The matches method takes an exchange as a parameter. This is nothing but a dictionary containing all the stocks that are available for the application.

We haven't talked about the `depends_on` method. This method just returns which stocks updates the rule depends on. This will be used later on to check the rule when any of those particular stocks get an update. For the `PriceRule`, it only depends on the stock that is passed in the initializer. An observant reader will notice that it returns a set (curly braces) and not a list.

Put this rule code in the file `rule.py` in the `stock_alerter` directory.

Here is how we would use the `PriceRule`:

```
>>> from datetime import datetime
>>> from stock_alerter.stock import Stock
>>> from stock_alerter.rule import PriceRule
>>>
>>> # First, create the exchange
>>> exchange = {"GOOG": Stock("GOOG"), "MSFT": Stock("MSFT")}
>>>
>>> # Next, create the rule, checking if GOOG price > 100
>>> rule = PriceRule("GOOG", lambda stock: stock.price > 100)
>>>
>>> # No updates? The rule is False
>>> rule.matches(exchange)
False
>>>
>>> # Price does not match the rule? Rule is False
>>> exchange["GOOG"].update(datetime(2014, 2, 13), 50)
>>> rule.matches(exchange)
False
>>>
>>> # Price matches the rule? Rule is True
>>> exchange["GOOG"].update(datetime(2014, 2, 13), 101)
>>> rule.matches(exchange)
True
>>>
```

This is what some of the tests would look like:

```python
class PriceRuleTest(unittest.TestCase):
    @classmethod
    def setUpClass(cls):
        goog = Stock("GOOG")
        goog.update(datetime(2014, 2, 10), 11)
        cls.exchange = {"GOOG": goog}

    def test_a_PriceRule_matches_when_it_meets_the_condition(self):
        rule = PriceRule("GOOG", lambda stock: stock.price > 10)
        self.assertTrue(rule.matches(self.exchange))

    def test_a_PriceRule_is_False_if_the_condition_is_not_met(self):
        rule = PriceRule("GOOG", lambda stock: stock.price < 10)
        self.assertFalse(rule.matches(self.exchange))

    def test_a_PriceRule_is_False_
        if_the_stock_is_not_in_the_exchange(self):
        rule = PriceRule("MSFT", lambda stock: stock.price > 10)
        self.assertFalse(rule.matches(self.exchange))

    def test_a_PriceRule_is_False_
        if_the_stock_hasnt_got_an_update_yet(self):
        self.exchange["AAPL"] = Stock("AAPL")
        rule = PriceRule("AAPL", lambda stock: stock.price > 10)
        self.assertFalse(rule.matches(self.exchange))

    def test_a_PriceRule_only_depends_on_its_stock(self):
        rule = PriceRule("MSFT", lambda stock: stock.price > 10)
        self.assertEqual({"MSFT"}, rule.depends_on())
```

One point to note is how we have used the `setupClass` method to do the setup. As discussed previously, this method is called just once for the whole series of tests. We use this method to set up the exchange and store it. Remember to put the `@classmethod` decorator on the `setupClass` method. We store the exchange in the class, and we can access it in the tests using `self.exchange`.

Otherwise, the tests are simply a matter of constructing a rule and checking the matches method.

>
> **A (very) quick primer on decorators**
> Decorators are functions that take a function as an input and return another function as an output. Python has a shorthand syntax by which we can say @decorator above a function or method and it will apply the decorator to that function. For more details, check the python documentation or a tutorial. A good one is http://simeonfranklin.com/blog/2012/jul/1/python-decorators-in-12-steps/.

Let us now look at another rule class, the AndRule. The AndRule is used when you want to compose two or more rules together, for example, AAPL > 10 AND GOOG > 15.

This is how we could write a test for it:

```
class AndRuleTest(unittest.TestCase):
    @classmethod
    def setUpClass(cls):
        goog = Stock("GOOG")
        goog.update(datetime(2014, 2, 10), 8)
        goog.update(datetime(2014, 2, 11), 10)
        goog.update(datetime(2014, 2, 12), 12)
        msft = Stock("MSFT")
        msft.update(datetime(2014, 2, 10), 10)
        msft.update(datetime(2014, 2, 11), 10)
        msft.update(datetime(2014, 2, 12), 12)
        redhat = Stock("RHT")
        redhat.update(datetime(2014, 2, 10), 7)
        cls.exchange = {"GOOG": goog, "MSFT": msft, "RHT": redhat}

    def test_an_AndRule_matches_
        if_all_component_rules_are_true(self):
        rule = AndRule(PriceRule("GOOG", lambda stock:
            stock.price > 8), PriceRule("MSFT", lambda stock:
            stock.price > 10))
        self.assertTrue(rule.matches(self.exchange))
```

One of the things about writing a test first is that it makes us think about how the class is going to be used.

For example, how should we pass in the various sub-rules to the AndRule? Should we have a method to set them? Should we pass them as a list? Should we pass them as individual parameters? This is a design decision and creating the test first allows us to actually write code as a user of our class and determine which is the best choice. In the test above, we have decided to pass in each sub-rule as a separate parameter to the AndRule constructor.

Now that the decision has been made, we can implement some code to pass the test:

```
class AndRule:
    def __init__(self, *args):
        self.rules = args


    def matches(self, exchange):
        return all([rule.matches(exchange) for rule in self.rules])
```

Here we can see how the test-first process helps drive the design of our code.

**The all function**

The all function is a built-in function that takes a list and returns True only if every element of that list is True.

# Exercise

It is now time to put our newly-learned skills into practice. Here is a new requirement to build into the Stock class:

- Sometimes, updates might come out of order and we might get an update for a newer timestamp, followed by an update for an older timestamp. This could be due to random network latency, or due to the fact that sometimes we might get updates from different sources and one might be slightly ahead of the other.

- The Stock class should be able to handle such cases, and the price attribute should return the latest price as per the timestamp.

- The is_increasing_trend should also process the latest three prices as per their timestamps.

Try your hand at implementing this requirement. Do not make any changes to the existing interfaces for these methods, but feel free to make any changes to the implementation as you require. Here are some things to think about:

- Does our existing design support this new feature? Do we need to make any changes to the current design?
- What kind of tests would we write for this requirement?
- After we get everything working, is there any clean up we can do to make the code more readable or maintainable?
- Do we need to change the existing tests after we make this change, or do they continue to work without any modifications?

By the end of the exercise, you should have all the existing tests passing, as well as any new ones that you wrote for this requirement. Once you are done, you can check *Appendix A, Answers to Exercises* for one possible solution to this exercise.

# Summary

In this chapter we took a more detailed look at the TDD cycle. We learnt about the Arrange-Act-Assert pattern, took a more detailed look at the various assertions that are provided, as well as some of the different ways of setting up tests and cleaning up afterwards. Finally, we looked at how to prevent tests from being too brittle and did a few basic refactorings.

# 3

# Code Smells and Refactoring

In the previous chapter, we went through the TDD cycle in a little more detail. In this chapter, we will look at the related concept of code smells and refactoring.

One of the biggest advantages of following a test-driven development process is that the tests that we write are always around to make sure that we don't break anything. This gives us a safety net to tinker with the code and make sure that it is easy to read, easy to maintain, and well written. Without tests, we always have a nagging doubt about whether we are about to break something, and more often than not we decide to leave things alone. This leads to the code decaying over time, until it is such a mess that no one wants to touch it anymore. The result is that it takes longer to implement new features, not only because the design is a mess, but also because we have to follow it with extensive testing to make sure none of the existing functionality has broken.

For this reason, it is vital that we do not skip the third step of the TDD cycle: refactoring.

 This code for this chapter starts at the point after the exercise in the previous chapter has been completed. See the *Appendix A, Answers to Exercises* for the changes done in the exercise, or download the starting point of the code for this chapter from `https://github.com/siddhi/test_driven_python`

# A dual crossover moving average

In the previous chapter, we wrote a method to check for an increasing trend. We will take that example forward in this chapter by developing a method to check for a dual crossover moving average.

A **dual crossover moving average (DMAC)** is a simple indicator to show the short-term trend of a stock compared to a long-term trend.

The following figure shows how the DMAC works:

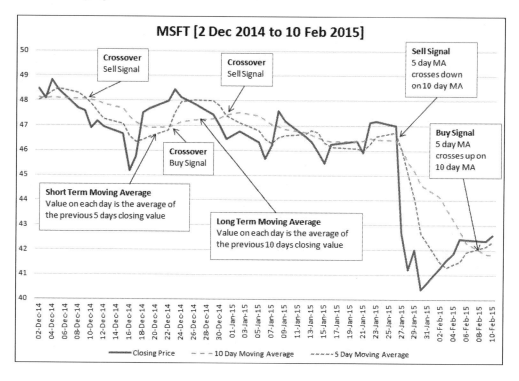

Consider a stock, with closing prices as shown above. First, we calculate two moving average trends. The short-term (5-day) moving average is calculated by taking the moving average for a short number of days. The long-term moving average is calculated by taking the moving average for a longer number of days, for example the moving average of the last 10 days.

When we plot the values of the long- term and short-term moving average graphs, we see that at certain points, the short-term graph crosses from below the long-term to above the long-term graph. This point represents a **Buy Signal**. At other points, the short-term crosses from above to below. This point represents a **Sell Signal**. At all other points, nothing should be done.

# Implementing the dual crossover moving average

What we are going to do is to implement a method `get_crossover_signal` for the `Stock` class. The following are the requirements for the method:

- The method takes a date as a parameter, and returns if there is any crossover on that date
- The method should return 1 if there is a **Buy Signal** (5-day moving average crosses 10-day moving average from below to above on that date)
- The method should return –1 if there is a **Sell Signal** (5-day moving average crosses 10-day moving average from above to below on that date)
- If there is no crossover, then the method returns 0 (**neutral** signal)
- The method should only take into account the closing price (the last update for the date), and not the opening or intermediate prices for the date
- If there are no updates for the date, then the method should use the previous closing price
- If there is not enough data to calculate the long-term moving average (we need closing prices for at least 11 days), then the method should return 0

# Identifying code smells

The following is an implementation that passes the tests (for a listing of the test cases, download the code for this chapter from `https://github.com/siddhi/test_driven_python`). The implementation uses the `timedelta` class from the `datetime` module, so you'll have to import it at the top of the file to get it to work.

```
def get_crossover_signal(self, on_date):
    cpl = []
    for i in range(11):
        chk = on_date.date() - timedelta(i)
        for price_event in reversed(self.price_history):
            if price_event.timestamp.date() > chk:
                pass
            if price_event.timestamp.date() == chk:
                cpl.insert(0, price_event)
                break
            if price_event.timestamp.date() < chk:
```

```
                    cpl.insert(0, price_event)
                    break


    # Return NEUTRAL signal
    if len(cpl) < 11:
        return 0


    # BUY signal
    if sum([update.price for update in cpl[-11:-1]])/10 \
            > sum([update.price for update in cpl[-6:-1]])/5 \
        and sum([update.price for update in cpl[-10:]])/10 \
            < sum([update.price for update in cpl[-5:]])/5:
                return 1


    # BUY signal
    if sum([update.price for update in cpl[-11:-1]])/10 \
            < sum([update.price for update in cpl[-6:-1]])/5 \
        and sum([update.price for update in cpl[-10:]])/10 \
            > sum([update.price for update in cpl[-5:]])/5:
                return -1


    # NEUTRAL signal
    return 0
```

While the above code implements the functionality, it is totally unreadable. This is what happens when the refactoring step is skipped. It will take a long time to understand when we come back to this code after some months to fix a bug or add functionality. Therefore, refactoring regularly is crucial.

What are the problems you can find with this code? The following are some problems:

- **Long method**: Long methods and classes are difficult to read and understand.
- **Unclear naming**: For instance, what is variable `cpl` supposed to be?
- **Complex conditionals**: The `if` conditions are quite complicated, and it is unclear what exactly they are checking for.
- **Bad comments**: None of the comments are descriptive and, in addition, two comments both say BUY signal. Obviously, one of them is wrong.

- **Magic constants**: In various places, the numbers 5, 10, –11, and so on are hard coded. Suppose we decide to change the long-term moving average to use a 20-day period, then where are the places we need to change? What is the possibility that we may miss one?

- **Code duplication**: Both the conditionals seem almost the same, with a very minor difference.

All these problems are generally referred to as code smells. **Code smells** are simple patterns that can be easily spotted and refactored to make code better. Sometimes, code smells can be rectified by doing a few simple changes. Other times, it may lead up to a change of the design itself.

# Refactoring

**Refactoring** is the process of cleaning up code or changing a design using a sequence of very small steps. No new functionality is added or removed during the refactoring process. The aim of refactoring is to make the code better by eliminating some code smell. There are many types of refactoring, from the extremely simple going up to much more complex refactorings. Let us apply some of these to the code above.

# The Rename Variable and Rename Method refactorings

These two are probably the two simplest refactorings. The names are self explanatory — the refactoring is to rename a variable or a method. Although simple, they are very important because poor variable and method names are very common code smells.

The following are the steps to apply the **Rename Variable** refactoring:

1. Run all the tests to make sure they are passing.
2. Change the name of the variable, and make the change in all the places where it is being used.
3. Run all the tests again to make sure we didn't break anything.

The **Rename Method** refactoring follows the following sequence of steps:

1. Run all the tests to make sure they are passing.
2. Change the name of the method, and make the change in all the places where this method is being called.
3. Run all the tests again.

Let us now apply the Rename Variable refactoring to our code. The `cpl` variable holds the list of the closing prices of the stock for the last 11 days. We should rename this to something more descriptive, like `closing_price_list`. Let us do this now:

1. Run the tests (a listing of the test cases is given in the *Exercise* section at the end of this chapter).

2. Rename `cpl` to `closing_price_list` at all places in the method.

3. Run the tests again. If there are any places where we forgot to rename the variable, then the tests will fail and we can fix it and run the tests again.

**Tests as a safety net**

Having a solid set of tests is critical before we do refactoring. This is because tests give us the confidence that we haven't broken anything during the refactoring. We will be running the tests multiple times during a refactoring as we proceed from step to step.

Let us now apply the Rename Variable refactoring to our code. The `cpl` variable holds the list of the closing prices of the stock for the last eleven days. We should rename this to something more descriptive, like `closing_price_list`.

A quick search and replace and the code now looks like this:

```python
def get_crossover_signal(self, on_date):
    closing_price_list = []
    for i in range(11):
        chk = on_date.date() - timedelta(i)
        for price_event in reversed(self.price_history):
            if price_event.timestamp.date() > chk:
                pass
            if price_event.timestamp.date() == chk:
                closing_price_list.insert(0, price_event)
                break
            if price_event.timestamp.date() < chk:
                closing_price_list.insert(0, price_event)
                break

    # Return NEUTRAL signal
    if len(closing_price_list) < 11:
```

```
        return 0


# BUY signal
if (sum([update.price
            for update in closing_price_list[-11:-1]])/10
        > sum([update.price
                for update in closing_price_list[-6:-1]])/5
    and sum([update.price
            for update in closing_price_list[-10:]])/10
        < sum([update.price
                for update in closing_price_list[-5:]])/5):
            return 1


# BUY signal
if (sum([update.price
            for update in closing_price_list[-11:-1]])/10
        < sum([update.price
            for update in closing_price_list[-6:-1]])/5
    and sum([update.price
                for update in closing_price_list[-10:]])/10
        > sum([update.price
                for update in closing_price_list[-5:]])/5):
            return -1


# NEUTRAL signal
return 0
```

# Commenting Styles

Next, let us look at the comments in the method. Generally speaking, comments are a code smell because they indicate that the code itself is not easy to read. Some comments, like the one in the code above, simply repeat what the code is doing. Often, we put in a comment like this because it is easier to do so rather than clean up the code. So, wherever we see comments, it is worthwhile exploring if a code cleanup might be required. The other problem with comments is that they can very easily go out of sync with the code. It is quite common that when we come back in the future to implement a new feature, we don't update the comments. It leads to a great deal of confusion when we try to understand code where the comments are not in sync with the code.

not all comments are bad. Helpful comments explain *why* a certain piece of code has been written that way. This is the information that cannot be deduced by just reading the code. Consider the following examples:

```
# Halve the price if age is 60 or above
if age >= 60:
    price = price * 0.5
```

```
# People aged 60 or above are eligible for senior citizen discount
if age >= 60:
    price = price * 0.5
```

```
if age >= SENIOR_CITIZEN_AGE:
    price = price * SENIOR_CITIZEN_DISCOUNT
```

The first example shows a comment that just repeats the code below it. There is no value added here by the comments. A cursory glance at the code will tell the reader exactly what the comment says.

The second example shows a much better comment. This comment doesn't repeat the code, but instead explains the rationale behind why this particular piece of code exists.

In the third example, the hardcoded numbers have been replaced by constants. In this example, the code is self-explanatory, so we can get rid of the comment altogether.

The three examples show the ideal process for writing comments. First, we see if we can make the code clearer in such a way that we don't need comments. If that is not possible, then write a comment around why the code has been written in a particular way. If you are tempted to write a comment about what a piece of code does, then stop and think about refactoring the code instead.

# Replace Magic Literals with Constants

As we saw in the previous example, replacing hardcoded values with constants accomplishes two things: first, should we need to change the values, we can do it at a single place, and, second, the constants are more descriptive and help make the code more readable.

The process for this refactoring is as follows:

1. Run the tests.

2. Create the constant and replace one hardcoded value with the constant.

3. Run the tests again.

4. Repeat steps 2 and 3 until all values are replaced with the constant.

Our method uses the timespan for the long-term moving average and the short-term moving average in all the calculations. We can create constants to identify these two values like the following:

```
class Stock:
    LONG_TERM_TIMESPAN = 10
    SHORT_TERM_TIMESPAN = 5
```

We can then use the constants in our method like the following:

```
def get_crossover_signal(self, on_date):
    closing_price_list = []
    NUM_DAYS = self.LONG_TERM_TIMESPAN + 1
    for i in range(NUM_DAYS):
        chk = on_date.date() - timedelta(i)
        for price_event in reversed(self.price_history):
            if price_event.timestamp.date() > chk:
                pass
            if price_event.timestamp.date() == chk:
                closing_price_list.insert(0, price_event)
                break
```

```
    if price_event.timestamp.date() < chk:
        closing_price_list.insert(0, price_event)
        break
```

Apart from the constants used in the calculation, we can also replace the return value with more descriptive Enum class. This is a new feature in Python 3.4 that we can use here.

 While Enum is a part of the standard library in Python 3.4, it has also been backported to earlier versions of Python. Download and install the enum34 package from PyPy if you are using an older Python version.

To do this, we first import Enum as follows:

```
from enum import Enum
```

We then create the enumeration class.

```
class StockSignal(Enum):
    buy = 1
    neutral = 0
    sell = -1
```

Finally, we can replace the return value with the enumeration:

```
    # NEUTRAL signal
    return StockSignal.neutral
```

With this change, we can also remove the comments above the return values, as the constants are descriptive enough.

# The Extract Method refactoring

Another way to make comments redundant is to take the code and put it in a method with a descriptive name. This also helps break down a long method into smaller methods that are easier to understand. The **Extract Method** refactoring is used for this purpose. The steps for the Extract Method refactoring are as follows:

1.  Run the existing tests.
2.  Identify the variables in the code block that we want to refactor, that are also used before the code block. These variables will need to be passed into our method as parameters.

3. Identify the variables in the code block that are used after the code block. These variables will be the return values from our method.

4. Create a method with a descriptive name that takes in the above variables as a parameter.

5. Make the new method return the appropriate values that are needed after the code block.

6. Move the code block into the method. Replace the lines with a call to the method.

7. Run the tests again.

Let us apply this refactoring to our method. This loop is used to create a list of closing prices for each of the previous eleven days:

```python
def _get_closing_price_list(self, on_date, num_days):
    closing_price_list = []
    for i in range(num_days):
        chk = on_date.date() - timedelta(i)
        for price_event in reversed(self.price_history):
            if price_event.timestamp.date() > chk:
                pass
            if price_event.timestamp.date() == chk:
                closing_price_list.insert(0, price_event)
                break
            if price_event.timestamp.date() < chk:
                closing_price_list.insert(0, price_event)
                break
    return closing_price_list
```

We can extract this code into a separate method. Here are the steps to do so:

1. First, we create a new method called _get_closing_price_list:

```python
def _get_closing_price_list(self, on_date, num_days):
    pass
```

This method takes two parameters because those values are used in the loop. Currently they are local variables, but once we extract the loop into this method, we will need to pass those values to the method.

2. We now cut the loop code from the main method and paste it into this new method:

```python
def _get_closing_price_list(self, on_date, num_days):
    closing_price_list = []
    for i in range(NUM_DAYS):
        chk = on_date.date() - timedelta(i)
        for price_event in reversed(self.price_history):
            if price_event.timestamp.date() > chk:
                pass
            if price_event.timestamp.date() == chk:
                closing_price_list.insert(0, price_event)
                break
            if price_event.timestamp.date() < chk:
                closing_price_list.insert(0, price_event)
                break
```

3. At this point, the loop still refers to the NUM_DAYS constant that was a local variable. We need to change this to use the value from the parameter. We also make this method return the closing_price_list:

```python
def _get_closing_price_list(self, on_date, num_days):
    closing_price_list = []
    for i in range(num_days):
        chk = on_date.date() - timedelta(i)
        for price_event in reversed(self.price_history):
            if price_event.timestamp.date() > chk:
                pass
            if price_event.timestamp.date() == chk:
                closing_price_list.insert(0, price_event)
                break
            if price_event.timestamp.date() < chk:
                closing_price_list.insert(0, price_event)
                break
    return closing_price_list
```

4. Finally, we put in a call to this method where the loop code originally was used:

```
def get_crossover_signal(self, on_date):
    NUM_DAYS = self.LONG_TERM_TIMESPAN + 1
    closing_price_list = \
        self._get_closing_price_list(on_date, NUM_DAYS)
```

Now we run the tests to make sure we didn't break anything. They should all pass.

Our code after refactoring looks like this:

```
def _get_closing_price_list(self, on_date, num_days):
    closing_price_list = []
    for i in range(num_days):
        chk = on_date.date() - timedelta(i)
        for price_event in reversed(self.price_history):
            if price_event.timestamp.date() > chk:
                pass
            if price_event.timestamp.date() == chk:
                closing_price_list.insert(0, price_event)
                break
            if price_event.timestamp.date() < chk:
                closing_price_list.insert(0, price_event)
                break
    return closing_price_list


def get_crossover_signal(self, on_date):
    NUM_DAYS = self.LONG_TERM_TIMESPAN + 1
    closing_price_list = \
        self._get_closing_price_list(on_date, NUM_DAYS)

    ...
```

# Replace Calculation with Temporary Variable

Let us now turn our attention to the conditional statements where we perform the checks for crossover.

The conditional is messy because we are doing many calculations and comparisons at the same time, which is hard to follow. We can clean this up by using temporary variables to store the calculation values and then using the variables in the conditionals.

In this refactoring, we are not using the variables for any purpose other than just being able to give a name to the calculations, and thereby making the code easier to read.

The following is how we do this refactoring:

1.  Run the tests.
2.  Take the calculation and assign it to a variable. Make the name of the variable explain the purpose of the calculation.
3.  Use the variable in the conditional.
4.  Run the tests.

Let us extract the four calculations in our conditional into variables:

```
long_term_series = closing_price_list[-self.LONG_TERM_TIMESPAN:]
prev_long_term_series = \
    closing_price_list[-self.LONG_TERM_TIMESPAN-1:-1]
short_term_series = closing_price_list[-self.SHORT_TERM_TIMESPAN:]
prev_short_term_series = \
    closing_price_list[-self.SHORT_TERM_TIMESPAN-1:-1]
```

We can then use these variables in the conditional:

```
if sum([update.price for update in prev_long_term_series])/10 \
    > sum([update.price for update in prev_short_term_series])/5 \
    and sum([update.price for update in long_term_series])/10 \
        < sum([update.price for update in short_term_series])/5:
            return StockSignal.buy
```

# Extract Conditional to Method

We can now turn our attention to the conditional. It isn't very clear as to what comparison is happening in the conditional. One way to handle this is to continue with the Replace Calculation with Temporary Variable refactoring above. Another option is to apply the **Extract Conditional to Method** refactoring. In this refactoring, we take the comparison and move it into its own method with a descriptive name.

The following are the steps for the refactoring:

1. Run the tests.
2. Take the entire conditional and move it into a method.
3. Call the method where the conditional was before.
4. Run the tests.

Here is the conditional code that we currently have:

```
if sum([update.price for update in prev_long_term_series])/10 \
    > sum([update.price for update in prev_short_term_series])/5 \
  and sum([update.price for update in long_term_series])/10 \
      < sum([update.price for update in short_term_series])/5:
          return StockSignal.buy
```

First we apply the Replace Calculation with Temporary Variable refactoring and extract the moving average calculation into a named variable:

```
long_term_ma = sum([update.price
                    for update in long_term_series])\
               /self.LONG_TERM_TIMESPAN
prev_long_term_ma = sum([update.price
                         for update in prev_long_term_series])\
               /self.LONG_TERM_TIMESPAN
short_term_ma = sum([update.price
                     for update in short_term_series])\
               /self.SHORT_TERM_TIMESPAN
prev_short_term_ma = sum([update.price
                          for update in prev_short_term_series])\
               /self.SHORT_TERM_TIMESPAN
```

Next the comparisons being made in the conditional can be extracted to methods like this:

```
def _is_short_term_crossover_below_to_above(self, prev_short_term_ma,
                                            prev_long_term_ma,
                                            short_term_ma,
                                            long_term_ma):
    return prev_long_term_ma > prev_short_term_ma \
        and long_term_ma < short_term_ma


def _is_short_term_crossover_above_to_below(self, prev_short_term_ma,
                                            prev_long_term_ma,
                                            short_term_ma,
                                            long_term_ma):
    return prev_long_term_ma < prev_short_term_ma \
        and long_term_ma > short_term_ma
```

We now call the method in the `if` statement, passing in our temporary variables as parameters:

```
if self._is_short_term_crossover_below_to_above(prev_short_term_ma,
                                                prev_long_term_ma,
                                                short_term_ma,
                                                long_term_ma):
        return StockSignal.buy


if self._is_short_term_crossover_above_to_below(prev_short_term_ma,
                                                prev_long_term_ma,
                                                short_term_ma,
                                                long_term_ma):
        return StockSignal.sell


return StockSignal.neutral
```

This is what the method looks like after the last few refactorings:

```
NUM_DAYS = self.LONG_TERM_TIMESPAN + 1
closing_price_list = self._get_closing_price_list(on_date, NUM_DAYS)

if len(closing_price_list) < NUM_DAYS:
    return StockSignal.neutral

long_term_series = closing_price_list[-self.LONG_TERM_TIMESPAN:]
prev_long_term_series = \
    closing_price_list[-self.LONG_TERM_TIMESPAN-1:-1]
short_term_series = closing_price_list[-self.SHORT_TERM_TIMESPAN:]
prev_short_term_series = \
    closing_price_list[-self.SHORT_TERM_TIMESPAN-1:-1]

long_term_ma = sum([update.price
                    for update in long_term_series])\
            /self.LONG_TERM_TIMESPAN
prev_long_term_ma = sum([update.price
                         for update in prev_long_term_series])\
            /self.LONG_TERM_TIMESPAN
short_term_ma = sum([update.price
                     for update in short_term_series])\
            /self.SHORT_TERM_TIMESPAN
prev_short_term_ma = sum([update.price
                          for update in prev_short_term_series])\
            /self.SHORT_TERM_TIMESPAN

if self._is_short_term_crossover_below_to_above(prev_short_term_ma,
                                                prev_long_term_ma,
                                                short_term_ma,
                                                long_term_ma):
            return StockSignal.buy

if self._is_short_term_crossover_above_to_below(prev_short_term_ma,
                                                prev_long_term_ma,
```

```
                                                short_term_ma,

                                                long_term_ma):

            return StockSignal.sell


    return StockSignal.neutral
```

# The DRY principle

One of the most important principles in writing good code is the DRY principle. **DRY** stands for **Don't Repeat Yourself**. If you ever find yourself writing the same (or similar) code in multiple places, there is a good chance that a refactoring will allow you to put that logic in once place and call it from each place that it is needed. It could be something as simple as moving the code into a function and calling the function from each place, or it could be a more complex refactoring.

Take another look at the conditionals that we just refactored:

```
def _is_short_term_crossover_below_to_above(self, prev_short_term_ma,
                                            prev_long_term_ma,

                                            short_term_ma,

                                            long_term_ma):
    return prev_long_term_ma > prev_short_term_ma \
        and long_term_ma < short_term_ma


def _is_short_term_crossover_above_to_below(self, prev_short_term_ma,
                                            prev_long_term_ma,

                                            short_term_ma,

                                            long_term_ma):
    return prev_long_term_ma < prev_short_term_ma \
        and long_term_ma > short_term_ma
```

We can see that they are almost the same. The only difference being that the comparisons are the other way around. Is there a way we can eliminate this code duplication?

One way is to change the order of the comparators in the first method:

```
def _is_short_term_crossover_below_to_above(self, prev_short_term_ma,
                                            prev_long_term_ma,
                                            short_term_ma,
                                            long_term_ma):
    return prev_short_term_ma < prev_long_term_ma \
        and short_term_ma > long_term_ma
```

Except for parameter names, it is now identical to the second method:

```
def _is_short_term_crossover_above_to_below(self, prev_short_term_ma,
                                            prev_long_term_ma,
                                            short_term_ma,
                                            long_term_ma):
    return prev_long_term_ma < prev_short_term_ma \
        and long_term_ma > short_term_ma
```

We can now merge both methods into one:

```
def _is_crossover_below_to_above(self, prev_ma, prev_reference_ma,
                                 current_ma, current_reference_ma):
    return prev_ma < prev_reference_ma \
        and current_ma > current_reference_ma
```

and call this single method in both conditionals:

```
if self._is_crossover_below_to_above(prev_short_term_ma,
                                     prev_long_term_ma,
                                     short_term_ma,
                                     long_term_ma):
        return StockSignal.buy


if self._is_crossover_below_to_above(prev_long_term_ma,
                                     prev_short_term_ma,
                                     long_term_ma,
                                     short_term_ma):
        return StockSignal.sell
```

Notice how the order of the short and long term parameters are exchanged between the two calls. The first checks that the short term moving average crosses the long term moving average from down to up. The second checks that the long term moving average crosses the short term moving average from down to up—this is the same as checking that the short term crosses from above to below. By doing the same check in both cases (below to above) and exchanging the parameters, we are able to eliminate the duplication in the code.

# Single Responsibility Principle

At this point, we have performed a number of local refactorings. These are refactorings such as moving code into or out of methods, pulling calculations into variables, and so on. These refactorings improve the readability of the code, but are mostly localized changes and don't affect the larger design.

From a design perspective, the most common reason that classes get cluttered is due to not following the **Single Responsibility Principle** (**SRP**). What this principle states is that a class should have a single, clear, coherent purpose. A class that tries to do too many different things is an indicator of a poor design.

Let us review whether the Stock class meets this criterion. The core responsibilities of the class are as follows:

- Keeping a history of price updates for a particular stock
- Checking whether the stock meets certain conditions

In addition, the class is also performing the following:

- Calculating a list of closing prices per day (or, more generally, code for handling a time series)
- Calculating the moving average for various points in time

The latter two responsibilities should be offloaded to a separate class.

# Extract Class

The **Extract Class** refactoring is used to take some functionality and move it into a separate class. This is easily the most commonly used design refactoring. It is an ideal refactoring to apply when we see that a class has become saddled with multiple responsibilities.

The following is what we want to do:

- Move all code relating to managing a time series into a `TimeSeries` class
- Move all code relating to moving averages into a `MovingAverage` class

The steps for performing an Extract Class refactoring are as follows:

1. Run all tests.
2. Create a new class.
3. Instantiate the new class in the `__init__` scope, or pass it in as a parameter.
4. Move one method from the source class to the new class. If the code to be moved is not in a method, then extract it to a local method using the Extract Method refactoring first.
5. Change all local calls to call the method in the new class instance.
6. Run the tests again.
7. Repeat steps 3 to 5 for each piece of functionality to be moved.

Let us now extract all the time series related functionality into a `TimeSeries` class.

First, we create a file called `timeseries.py` in the `stock_alerter` directory. We'll create our class here.

Next, we'll create an empty `TimeSeries` class in `timeseries.py` as follows:

```
class TimeSeries:
    pass
```

So far, we've been using `price_history`, a list, to store the price history. We now want to store all this information in our `TimeSeries` class. We'll make this transition step by step. The first step is to add an instance variable to the `Stock` class as follows:

```
def __init__(self, symbol):
    self.symbol = symbol
    self.price_history = []
    self.history = TimeSeries()
```

Remember to import `TimeSeries` at the top of the file before making this change. Now we can migrate the update functionality into the `TimeSeries` class as follows:

```
import bisect
import collections


Update = collections.namedtuple("Update", ["timestamp", "value"])


class TimeSeries:
    def __init__(self):
        self.series = []


    def update(self, timestamp, value):
        bisect.insort_left(self.series, Update(timestamp, value))
```

Once migrated, we make a call to the new method in the `Stock` class as follows:

```
    def update(self, timestamp, price):
        if price < 0:
            raise ValueError("price should not be negative")
        bisect.insort_left(self.price_history,
            PriceEvent(timestamp, price))
        self.history.update(timestamp, price)
```

Notice how we have just added the call to the timeseries, but we haven't removed the old call that updates `self.price_history`. This is because this list is still used directly in other places. By not removing this line yet, we don't break any functionality. All the tests still pass. Once we are done with the migration, we'll come back and remove this line.

Now we need to change the price and `is_increasing_trend` methods to stop using `self.price_history` and start using the time series class. This is what they look like currently:

```
def price(self):
    return self.price_history[-1].price \
        if self.price_history else None


def is_increasing_trend(self):
    return self.price_history[-3].price < \
        self.price_history[-2].price < self.price_history[-1].price
```

Our next step is to add a dictionary access method to `TimeSeries`:

```
class TimeSeries:
    def __getitem__(self, index):
        return self.series[index]
```

This enables us to change the `Stock.price` and `Stock.is_increasing_trend` methods to use the `TimeSeries` class instead of accessing `self.price_history`.

```
    def price(self):
        try:
            return self.history[-1].value
        except IndexError:
            return None


    def is_increasing_trend(self):
        return self.history[-3].value < \
            self.history[-2].value < self.history[-1].value
```

We should run the tests again to check that the new implementation of `Stock.price` and `Stock.is_increasing_trend` still work as expected. All 21 tests should still be passing.

# Move Method to Class

There is one final place where `self.price_history` is used, and this is in the `_get_closing_price_list` method. Instead of replacing the usage of `self.price_history`, we are instead going to move the whole method into the `TimeSeries` class. This is the **Move Method to Class** refactoring.

To do this refactoring, we will do the following:

1. Run the tests.
2. Move the method to the target class. If the method uses any instance variables, then we need to add them to the parameter list.
3. Replace all calls to use the method in the other class, adding any new parameters that need to be passed.
4. Some callers may not have a reference to the target class. In that case, we need to instantiate the object in the `__init__` scope or pass a reference to it as a parameter.
5. Run the tests again.

Usually, at the end of this refactoring, we need to do some further local refactoring in the target class. So, some of those extra parameters that were added might need to be moved elsewhere or changed. Some parameters might be added to the initializer and callers modified appropriately.

The following example will make this clearer. Let us start by moving the _get_ closing_price_list method to the TimeSeries class. Since this will be a public method in the new class, we can drop the initial underscore in the name.

```
class TimeSeries:
    def get_closing_price_list(self, on_date, num_days,
price_history):
        closing_price_list = []
        for i in range(num_days):
            chk = on_date.date() - timedelta(i)
            for price_event in reversed(price_history):
                if price_event.timestamp.date() > chk:
                    pass
                if price_event.timestamp.date() == chk:
                    closing_price_list.insert(0, price_event)
                    break
                if price_event.timestamp.date() < chk:
                    closing_price_list.insert(0, price_event)
                    break
        return closing_price_list
```

Notice the extra price_history parameter that we added to this method. The original method used the self.price_history variable. Since this is an instance variable of the Stock class, it is not available in the TimeSeries class. To fix that, we pass in the price_history as a parameter and use this in the method.

The call from the Stock class now looks like the following:

```
def get_crossover_signal(self, on_date):
    NUM_DAYS = self.LONG_TERM_TIMESPAN + 1
    closing_price_list =
        self.history.get_closing_price_list(on_date, NUM_DAYS,
        self.price_history)
```

We run the tests at this point to validate that all the tests are still passing.

Once we verify that the tests are passing, we can now go back and remove the extra parameter that we added. The `TimeSeries` class has its own instance variable `self.series` that contains the price history. We can use this variable in the method and remove the extra parameter. The method now becomes as follows:

```python
def get_closing_price_list(self, on_date, num_days):
    closing_price_list = []
    for i in range(num_days):
        chk = on_date.date() - timedelta(i)
        for price_event in reversed(self.series):
            if price_event.timestamp.date() > chk:
                pass
            if price_event.timestamp.date() == chk:
                closing_price_list.insert(0, price_event)
                break
            if price_event.timestamp.date() < chk:
                closing_price_list.insert(0, price_event)
                break
    return closing_price_list
```

And the call becomes as follows:

```python
def get_crossover_signal(self, on_date):
    NUM_DAYS = self.LONG_TERM_TIMESPAN + 1
    closing_price_list = \
        self.history.get_closing_price_list(on_date, NUM_DAYS)
```

Run the tests again to check that everything is working, as shown in the following:

```
==================================================================
ERROR: test_with_upward_crossover_returns_buy (stock_alerter.stock.
StockCrossOverSignalTest)
------------------------------------------------------------------
Traceback (most recent call last):
  File "c:\Projects\tdd_with_python\src\stock_alerter\stock.py", line
239, in test_with_upward_crossover_returns_buy
    self.goog.get_crossover_signal(date_to_check))
  File "c:\Projects\tdd_with_python\src\stock_alerter\stock.py", line 63,
in get_crossover_signal
    for update in long_term_series])\
```

```
   File "c:\Projects\tdd_with_python\src\stock_alerter\stock.py", line 63,
in <listcomp>
     for update in long_term_series])\
AttributeError: 'Update' object has no attribute 'price'


Ran 21 tests in 0.018s


FAILED (errors=7)
```

Oops! Looks like some of the tests are failing!

The problem is that the updates stored in `self.price_history` use the `price` attribute to refer to the price, but the `timeseries` module calls it value. So, we need to change the places where we calculate the moving average and replace price with value. With that change, the tests pass again and our moving average calculation now looks like the following:

```
long_term_ma = sum([update.value
                       for update in long_term_series])\
              /self.LONG_TERM_TIMESPAN
prev_long_term_ma = sum([update.value
                            for update in
                                prev_long_term_series])\
                   /self.LONG_TERM_TIMESPAN
short_term_ma = sum([update.value
                        for update in short_term_series])\
               /self.SHORT_TERM_TIMESPAN
prev_short_term_ma = sum([update.value
                             for update in
                                 prev_short_term_series])\
                    /self.SHORT_TERM_TIMESPAN
```

The above code is the same as before except that we now use `update.value` instead of `update.price`.

Now, `price_history` is no longer used anywhere in the `Stock` class, so we can remove it from the class. We can also remove the `PriceEvent` named tuple as well as any unused imports. The initializer and update method after those changes are as follows:

```
class Stock:
    LONG_TERM_TIMESPAN = 10
```

```
SHORT_TERM_TIMESPAN = 5


def __init__(self, symbol):
    self.symbol = symbol
    self.history = TimeSeries()


def update(self, timestamp, price):
    if price < 0:
        raise ValueError("price should not be negative")
    self.history.update(timestamp, price)
```

With this change, our Extract Class refactoring is complete.

# The importance of tests

The Extract Class refactoring shows the importance of having a good unit test suite as well as running it frequently during the refactoring. It is easy to overlook small things when moving code around, which could end up breaking the code. By running the tests often, we know immediately when we break something. This makes it easy to fix the mistake. Had we done the whole refactoring before running the tests, it would have not been clear which step in the refactoring broke the tests, and we would have to go back and debug the whole refactoring.

One more thing that we need to do is to adjust the tests after the refactoring is complete. In some refactorings, such as Extract Class, we may find that we have to also move tests to the new class. For instance, if we had any tests for the _get_closing_ price_list method, then we would move those tests over to the TimeSeries class. In this case, since the method was not public, we didn't write tests for them and we didn't have anything to move.

After the refactoring, that method has become a public method on the TimeSeries class, and it currently doesn't have any tests. It is a good idea to go back and write some tests for the method.

# Exercise

Just as we extracted the time series code into its own class, we can also extract the moving average code into a separate class. Try doing this refactoring as an exercise. Once you are done, check out the Appendix for a walkthrough of one possible solution.

# Wrapping up

Here is the algorithm for calculating the DMAC in pseudocode:

1.  Calculate the short term and long term moving averages.
2.  If the short term crosses the long term from bottom to top, then *buy*.
3.  If the long term crosses the short term from bottom to top, then *sell*.
4.  Otherwise do nothing.

This is the code we started with, which passed all the tests:

```python
def get_crossover_signal(self, on_date):
    cpl = []
    for i in range(11):
        chk = on_date.date() - timedelta(i)
        for price_event in reversed(self.price_history):
            if price_event.timestamp.date() > chk:
                pass
            if price_event.timestamp.date() == chk:
                cpl.insert(0, price_event)
                break
            if price_event.timestamp.date() < chk:
                cpl.insert(0, price_event)
                break

    # Return NEUTRAL signal
    if len(cpl) < 11:
        return 0

    # BUY signal
    if sum([update.price for update in cpl[-11:-1]])/10 \
            > sum([update.price for update in cpl[-6:-1]])/5 \
        and sum([update.price for update in cpl[-10:]])/10 \
            < sum([update.price for update in cpl[-5:]])/5:
                return 1

    # BUY signal
    if sum([update.price for update in cpl[-11:-1]])/10 \
```

```
            < sum([update.price for update in cpl[-6:-1]])/5 \
        and sum([update.price for update in cpl[-10:]])/10 \
            > sum([update.price for update in cpl[-5:]])/5:
                return -1


    # NEUTRAL signal
    return 0
```

After the moving average code is extracted into its own class (see the exercise above to try this, or the *Appendix A, Answers to Exercises* to see one solution of how we got here), this is what the get_crossover_signal method looks like:

```
def get_crossover_signal(self, on_date):
    long_term_ma = MovingAverage(self.history, self.LONG_TERM_TIMESPAN)
    short_term_ma = MovingAverage(self.history, self.SHORT_TERM_TIMESPAN)


    try:
        if self._is_crossover_below_to_above(
                on_date,
                short_term_ma,
                long_term_ma):
            return StockSignal.buy


        if self._is_crossover_below_to_above(
                on_date,
                long_term_ma,
                short_term_ma):
            return StockSignal.sell
    except NotEnoughDataException:
        return StockSignal.neutral


    return StockSignal.neutral
```

The difference is clear. The refactored code reads just like the pseudocode above, with an almost 1:1 correspondence. A person who knows the algorithm will instantly know what this method is doing. We don't need to write a line of comments to make this readable. We cannot say the same for the code we started with.

The new code is only 9 statements long and delegates all the non-core functionality to the `TimeSeries` and `MovingAverage` classes. These classes are themselves quite short, and easy to understand. Overall, the refactoring has made a huge improvement in the quality of the code.

The best part? We made small changes and always had the tests as a safety net so we were sure we didn't break anything. Without the tests, we could not have undertaken these refactorings—the risk of breaking code is just too large. In fact, while writing the code that you see in this chapter, I did break the tests several times. Fortunately the tests were there and the errors were fixed in minutes.

One might ask about the time taken to perform all the refactorings we have gone through so far. This chapter looks quite huge and intimidating, but once we are comfortable with the techniques, it would take only about 30 to 60 minutes to perform all these refactorings.

# Summary

In this chapter, you looked at some of the most common code smells as well as the most common refactorings to fix them. You saw, step by step, how to perform each of the refactorings on our project and how having a good test suite enables us to perform such refactorings with confidence. Test-driven development and refactoring go hand in hand and are invaluable tools in any developer's toolbox. In the next chapter, we will take a look at testing code interactions using mock objects.

# 4
# Using Mock Objects to Test Interactions

Having looked at the `Rule` and `Stock` classes, let us now turn our attention to the `Event` class. The `Event` class is very simple: receivers can register with the event to be notified when the event occurs. When the event fires, all the receivers are notified of the event.

A more detailed description is as follows:

- Event classes have a `connect` method, which takes a method or function to be called when the event fires
- When the `fire` method is called, all the registered callbacks are called with the same parameters that are passed to the `fire` method

Writing tests for the `connect` method is fairly straightforward—we just need to check that the receivers are being stored properly. But, how do we write the tests for the fire method? This method does not change any state or store any value that we can assert on. The main responsibility of this method is to call other methods. How do we test that this is being done correctly?

This is where mock objects come into the picture. Unlike ordinary unit tests that assert on object *state*, mock objects are used to test that the *interactions* between multiple objects occurs as it should.

# Hand writing a simple mock

To start with, let us look at the code for the Event class so that we can understand what the tests need to do. The following code is in the file event.py in the source directory:

```
class Event:
    """A generic class that provides signal/slot functionality"""

    def __init__(self):
        self.listeners = []

    def connect(self, listener):
        self.listeners.append(listener)

    def fire(self, *args, **kwargs):
        for listener in self.listeners:
            listener(*args, **kwargs)
```

The way this code works is fairly simple. Classes that want to get notified of the event should call the connect method and pass a function. This will register the function for the event. Then, when the event is fired using the fire method, all the registered functions will be notified of the event. The following is a walk-through of how this class is used:

```
>>> def handle_event(num):
...     print("I got number {0}".format(num))
...
>>> event = Event()
>>> event.connect(handle_event)
>>> event.fire(3)
I got number 3
>>> event.fire(10)
I got number 10
```

As you can see, every time the fire method is called, all the functions that registered with the connect method get called with the given parameters.

So, how do we test the `fire` method? The walk-through above gives a hint. What we need to do is to create a function, register it using the `connect` method, and then verify that the method got notified when the `fire` method was called. The following is one way to write such a test:

```python
import unittest
from ..event import Event


class EventTest(unittest.TestCase):
    def test_a_listener_is_notified_when_an_event_is_raised(self):
        called = False
        def listener():
            nonlocal called
            called = True

        event = Event()
        event.connect(listener)
        event.fire()
        self.assertTrue(called)
```

Put this code into the `test_event.py` file in the tests folder and run the test. The test should pass. The following is what we are doing:

1. First, we create a variable named called and set it to `False`.
2. Next, we create a dummy function. When the function is called, it sets called to `True`.
3. Finally, we connect the dummy function to the event and fire the event.
4. If the dummy function was successfully called when the event was fired, then the `called` variable would be changed to `True`, and we assert that the variable is indeed what we expected.

The dummy function we created above is an example of a mock. A **mock** is simply an object that is substituted for a real object in the test case. The mock then records some information such as whether it was called, what parameters were passed, and so on, and we can then assert that the mock was called as expected.

Talking about parameters, we should write a test that checks that the parameters are being passed correctly. The following is one such test:

```
def test_a_listener_is_passed_right_parameters(self):
    params = ()
    def listener(*args, **kwargs):
        nonlocal params
        params = (args, kwargs)
    event = Event()
    event.connect(listener)
    event.fire(5, shape="square")
    self.assertEquals(((5, ), {"shape":"square"}), params)
```

This test is the same as the previous one, except that it saves the parameters that are then used in the assert to verify that they were passed properly.

At this point, we can see some repetition coming up in the way we set up the mock function and then save some information about the call. We can extract this code into a separate class as follows:

```
class Mock:
    def __init__(self):
        self.called = False
        self.params = ()

    def __call__(self, *args, **kwargs):
        self.called = True
        self.params = (args, kwargs)
```

Once we do this, we can use our Mock class in our tests as follows:

```
class EventTest(unittest.TestCase):
    def test_a_listener_is_notified_when_an_event_is_raised(self):
        listener = Mock()
        event = Event()
        event.connect(listener)
        event.fire()
```

```
        self.assertTrue(listener.called)


    def test_a_listener_is_passed_right_parameters(self):
        listener = Mock()
        event = Event()
        event.connect(listener)
        event.fire(5, shape="square")
        self.assertEquals(((5, ), {"shape": "square"}),
            listener.params)
```

What we have just done is to create a simple mocking class that is quite lightweight and good for simple uses. However, there are often times when we need much more advanced functionality, such as mocking a series of calls or checking the order of specific calls. Fortunately, Python has us covered with the unittest.mock module that is supplied as a part of the standard library.

# Using the Python mocking framework

The unittest.mock module provided by Python is an extremely powerful mocking framework, yet at the same time it is very easy to use.

Let us redo our tests using this library. First, we need to import the mock module at the top of our file as follows:

```
from unittest import mock
```

Next, we rewrite our first test as follows:

```
class EventTest(unittest.TestCase):
    def test_a_listener_is_notified_when_an_event_is_raised(self):
        listener = mock.Mock()
        event = Event()
        event.connect(listener)
        event.fire()
        self.assertTrue(listener.called)
```

The only change that we've made is to replace our own custom Mock class with the mock.Mock class provided by Python. That is it. With that single line change, our test is now using the inbuilt mocking class.

The `unittest.mock.Mock` class is the core of the Python mocking framework. All we need to do is to instantiate the class and pass it in where it is required. The mock will record if it was called in the `called` instance variable.

How do we check that the right parameters were passed? Let us look at the rewrite of the second test as follows:

```
def test_a_listener_is_passed_right_parameters(self):
    listener = mock.Mock()
    event = Event()
    event.connect(listener)
    event.fire(5, shape="square")
    listener.assert_called_with(5, shape="square")
```

The mock object automatically records the parameters that were passed in. We can assert on the parameters by using the `assert_called_with` method on the `mock` object. The method will raise an assertion error if the parameters don't match what was expected. In case we are not interested in testing the parameters (maybe we just want to check that the method was called), then we can pass the value `mock.ANY`. This value will match any parameter passed.

There is a subtle difference in the way normal assertions are called compared to assertions on mocks. Normal assertions are defined as a part of the `unittest.Testcase` class. Since our tests inherit from that class, we call the assertions on self, for example, `self.assertEquals`. On the other hand, the mock assertion methods are a part of the `mock` object, so you call them on the mock object, for example, `listener.assert_called_with`.

Mock objects have the following four assertions available out of the box:

- `assert_called_with`: This method asserts that the last call was made with the given parameters

- `assert_called_once_with`: This assertion checks that the method was called exactly once and was with the given parameters

- `assert_any_call`: This checks that the given call was made at some point during the execution

- `assert_has_calls`: This assertion checks that a list of calls occurred

The four assertions are very subtly different, and that shows up when the mock has been called more than one. The `assert_called_with` method only checks the last call, so if there was more than one call, then the previous calls will not be asserted. The `assert_any_call` method will check if a call with the given parameters occurred anytime during execution. The `assert_called_once_with` assertion asserts for a single call, so if the mock was called more than once during execution, then this assert would fail. The `assert_has_calls` assertion can be used to assert that a set of calls with the given parameters occurred. Note that there might have been more calls than what we checked for in the assertion, but the assertion would still pass as long as the given calls are present.

Let us take a closer look at the `assert_has_calls` assertion. Here is how we can write the same test using this assertion:

```
def test_a_listener_is_passed_right_parameters(self):
    listener = mock.Mock()
    event = Event()
    event.connect(listener)
    event.fire(5, shape="square")
    listener.assert_has_calls([mock.call(5, shape="square")])
```

The mocking framework internally uses `_Call` objects to record calls. The `mock.call` function is a helper to create these objects. We just call it with the expected parameters to create the required call objects. We can then use these objects in the `assert_has_calls` assertion to assert that the expected call occurred.

This method is useful when the mock was called multiple times and we want to assert only some of the calls.

# Mocking objects

While testing the `Event` class, we only needed to mock out single functions. A more common use of mocking is to mock a class.

> The rest of this chapter builds on `test_driven_python-CHAPTER4_PART2` of the code bundle. Download it from from `https://github.com/siddhi/test_driven_python/archive/CHAPTER4_PART2.zip`.

Take a look at the implementation of the `Alert` class in the following:

```
class Alert:
    """Maps a Rule to an Action, and triggers the action if the rule
    matches on any stock update"""

    def __init__(self, description, rule, action):
        self.description = description
        self.rule = rule
        self.action = action

    def connect(self, exchange):
        self.exchange = exchange
        dependent_stocks = self.rule.depends_on()
        for stock in dependent_stocks:
            exchange[stock].updated.connect(self.check_rule)

    def check_rule(self, stock):
        if self.rule.matches(self.exchange):
            self.action.execute(self.description)
```

Let's break down how this class works as follows:

- The `Alert` class takes a `Rule` and an `Action` in the initializer.
- When the `connect` method is called, it takes all the dependent stocks and connects to their `updated` event.
- The `updated` event is an instance of the `Event` class that we saw earlier. Each `Stock` class has an instance of this event, and it is fired whenever a new update is made to that stock.
- The listener for this event is the `self.check_rule` method of the `Alert` class.
- In this method, the alert checks if the new update caused a rule to be matched.
- If the rule matched, it calls the execute method on the `Action`. Otherwise, nothing happens.

This class has a few requirements, as shown in the following, that need to be met. Each of these needs to be made into a unit test.

- If a stock is updated, the class should check if the rule matches
- If the rule matches, then the corresponding action should be executed
- If the rule doesn't match, then nothing happens

There are a number of different ways in which we could test this; let us go through some of the options.

The first option is not to use mocks at all. We could create a rule, hook it up to a test action, and then update the stock and verify that the action was executed. The following is what such a test would look like:

```
import unittest
from datetime import datetime
from unittest import mock


from ..alert import Alert
from ..rule import PriceRule
from ..stock import Stock


class TestAction:
    executed = False


    def execute(self, description):
        self.executed = True


class AlertTest(unittest.TestCase):
    def test_action_is_executed_when_rule_matches(self):
        exchange = {"GOOG": Stock("GOOG")}
        rule = PriceRule("GOOG", lambda stock: stock.price > 10)
        action = TestAction()
        alert = Alert("sample alert", rule, action)
        alert.connect(exchange)
        exchange["GOOG"].update(datetime(2014, 2, 10), 11)
        self.assertTrue(action.executed)
```

This is the most straightforward option, but it requires a bit of code to set up and there is the `TestAction` that we need to create just for the test case.

Instead of creating a test action, we could instead replace it with a mock action. We can then simply assert on the mock that it got executed. The following code shows this variation of the test case:

```
def test_action_is_executed_when_rule_matches(self):
    exchange = {"GOOG": Stock("GOOG")}
    rule = PriceRule("GOOG", lambda stock: stock.price > 10)
    action = mock.MagicMock()
    alert = Alert("sample alert", rule, action)
    alert.connect(exchange)
    exchange["GOOG"].update(datetime(2014, 2, 10), 11)
    action.execute.assert_called_with("sample alert")
```

A couple of observations about this test:

If you notice, alert is not the usual `Mock` object that we have been using so far, but a `MagicMock` object. A `MagicMock` object is like a `Mock` object but it has special support for Python's magic methods which are present on all classes, such as `__str__`, `hasattr`. If we don't use `MagicMock`, we may sometimes get errors or strange behavior if the code uses any of these methods. The following example illustrates the difference:

```
>>> from unittest import mock
>>> mock_1 = mock.Mock()
>>> mock_2 = mock.MagicMock()
>>> len(mock_1)
Traceback (most recent call last):
  File "<stdin>", line 1, in <module>
TypeError: object of type 'Mock' has no len()
>>> len(mock_2)
0
>>>
```

In general, we will be using `MagicMock` in most places where we need to mock a class. Using `Mock` is a good option when we need to mock stand alone functions, or in rare situations where we specifically don't want a default implementation for the magic methods.

The other observation about the test is the way methods are handled. In the test above, we created a mock action object, but we didn't specify anywhere that this mock class should contain an `execute` method and how it should behave. In fact, we don't need to. When a method or attribute is accessed on a mock object, Python conveniently creates a mock method and adds it to the mock class. Therefore, when the `Alert` class calls the `execute` method on our mock action object, that method is added to our mock action. We can then check that the method was called by asserting on `action.execute.called`.

The downside of Python's behavior of automatically creating mock methods when they are accessed is that a typo or change in interface can go unnoticed.

For example, suppose we rename the `execute` method in all the `Action` classes to run. But if we run our test cases, it still passes. Why does it pass? Because the `Alert` class calls the `execute` method, and the test only checks that the `execute` method was called, which it was. The test does not know that the name of the method has been changed in all the real `Action` implementations and that the `Alert` class will not work when integrated with the actual actions.

To avoid this problem, Python supports using another class or object as a specification. When a specification is given, the mock object only creates the methods that are present in the specification. All other method or attribute accesses will raise an error.

Specifications are passed to the mock at initialization time via the `spec` parameter. Both the `Mock` as well as `MagicMock` classes support setting a specification. The following code example shows the difference when a `spec` parameter is set compared to a default `Mock` object:

```
>>> from unittest import mock
>>> class PrintAction:
...        def run(self, description):
...            print("{0} was executed".format(description))
...
...

>>> mock_1 = mock.Mock()
>>> mock_1.execute("sample alert") # Does not give an error
<Mock name='mock.execute()' id='54481752'>

>>> mock_2 = mock.Mock(spec=PrintAction)
>>> mock_2.execute("sample alert") # Gives an error
Traceback (most recent call last):
  File "<stdin>", line 1, in <module>
```

```
File "C:\Python34\lib\unittest\mock.py", line 557, in __getattr__
    raise AttributeError("Mock object has no attribute %r" % name)
AttributeError: Mock object has no attribute 'execute'
```

Notice in the above example that `mock_1` goes ahead and executes the `execute` method without any error, even though the method has been renamed in the `PrintAction`. On the other hand, by giving a spec, the method call to the nonexistent `execute` method raises an exception.

# Mocking return values

The second variant above showed how we could use a mock `Action` class in the test instead of a real one. In the same way, we can also use a mock rule instead of creating a `PriceRule` in the test. The alert calls the rule to see whether the new stock update caused the rule to be matched. What the alert does depends on whether the rule returned `True` or `False`.

All the mocks we've created so far have not had to return a value. We were just interested in whether the right call was made or not. If we mock the rule, then we will have to configure it to return the right value for the test. Fortunately, Python makes that very simple to do.

All we have to do is to set the return value as a parameter in the constructor to the mock object as follows:

```
>>> matches = mock.Mock(return_value=True)
>>> matches()
True
>>> matches(4)
True
>>> matches(4, "abcd")
True
```

As we can see above, the mock just blindly returns the set value, irrespective of the parameters. Even the type or number of parameters is not considered. We can use the same procedure to set the return value of a method in a mock object as follows:

```
>>> rule = mock.MagicMock()
>>> rule.matches = mock.Mock(return_value=True)
>>> rule.matches()
True
>>>
```

There is another way to set the return value, which is very convenient when dealing with methods in mock objects. Each mock object has a `return_value` attribute. We simply set this attribute to the return value and every call to the mock will return that value, as shown in the following:

```
>>> from unittest import mock
>>> rule = mock.MagicMock()
>>> rule.matches.return_value = True
>>> rule.matches()
True
>>>
```

In the example above, the moment we access `rule.matches`, Python automatically creates a mock `matches` object and puts it in the `rule` object. This allows us to directly set the return value in one statement without having to create a mock for the `matches` method.

Now that we've seen how to set the return value, we can go ahead and change our test to use a mocked rule object, as shown in the following:

```
def test_action_is_executed_when_rule_matches(self):
    exchange = {"GOOG": Stock("GOOG")}
    rule = mock.MagicMock(spec=PriceRule)
    rule.matches.return_value = True
    rule.depends_on.return_value = {"GOOG"}
    action = mock.MagicMock()
    alert = Alert("sample alert", rule, action)
    alert.connect(exchange)
    exchange["GOOG"].update(datetime(2014, 2, 10), 11)
    action.execute.assert_called_with("sample alert")
```

There are two calls that the `Alert` makes to the rule: one to the `depends_on` method and the other to the matches method. We set the return value for both of them and the test passes.

>  In case no return value is explicitly set for a call, the default return value is to return a new mock object. The mock object is different for each method that is called, but is consistent for a particular method. This means if the same method is called multiple times, the same mock object will be returned each time.

# Mocking side effects

Finally, we come to the Stock class. This is the final dependency of the Alert class. We're currently creating Stock objects in our test, but we could replace it with a mock object just like we did for the Action and PriceRule classes.

The Stock class is again slightly different in behavior from the other two mock objects. The update method doesn't just return a value—it's primary behavior in this test is to trigger the updated event. Only if this event is triggered will the rule check occur.

In order to do this, we must tell our mock stock class to fire the event when the update event is called. Mock objects have a side_effect attribute to enable us to do just this.

There are many reasons we might want to set a side effect. Some of them are as follows:

- We may want to call another method, like in the case of the Stock class, which needs to fire the event when the update method is called.

- To raise an exception: this is particularly useful when testing error situations. Some errors such as a network timeout might be very difficult to simulate, and it is better to test using a mock that simply raises the appropriate exception.

- To return multiple values: these may be different values each time the mock is called, or specific values, depending on the parameters passed.

Setting the side effect is just like setting the return value. The only difference is that the side effect is a lambda function. When the mock is executed, the parameters are passed to the lambda function and the lambda is executed. The following is how we would use this with a mocked out Stock class:

```python
def test_action_is_executed_when_rule_matches(self):
    goog = mock.MagicMock(spec=Stock)
    goog.updated = Event()
    goog.update.side_effect = lambda date, value:
            goog.updated.fire(self)
    exchange = {"GOOG": goog}
    rule = mock.MagicMock(spec=PriceRule)
    rule.matches.return_value = True
    rule.depends_on.return_value = {"GOOG"}
    action = mock.MagicMock()
    alert = Alert("sample alert", rule, action)
```

```
alert.connect(exchange)
exchange["GOOG"].update(datetime(2014, 2, 10), 11)
action.execute.assert_called_with("sample alert")
```

So what is going on in that test?

1. First, we create a mock of the `Stock` class instead of using the real one.

2. Next, we add in the `updated` event. We need to do this because the `Stock` class creates the attribute at runtime in the __init__ scope. Because the attribute is set dynamically, `MagicMock` does not pick up the attribute from the `spec` parameter. We are setting an actual `Event` object here. We could set it as a mock as well, but it is probably overkill to do that.

3. Finally, we set the side effect for the `update` method in the mock stock object. The lambda takes the two parameters that the method does. In this particular example, we just want to fire the event, so the parameters aren't used in the lambda. In other cases, we might want to perform different actions based on the values of the parameters. Setting the `side_effect` attribute allows us to do that.

Just like with the `return_value` attribute, the `side_effect` attribute can also be set in the constructor.

Run the test and it should pass.

The `side_effect` attribute can also be set to an exception or a list. If it is set to an exception, then the given exception will be raised when the mock is called, as shown in the following:

```
>>> m = mock.Mock()
>>> m.side_effect = Exception()
>>> m()
Traceback (most recent call last):
  File "<stdin>", line 1, in <module>
  File "C:\Python34\lib\unittest\mock.py", line 885, in __call__
    return _mock_self._mock_call(*args, **kwargs)
  File "C:\Python34\lib\unittest\mock.py", line 941, in _mock_call
    raise effect
Exception
```

If it is set to a list, then the mock will return the next element of the list each time it is called. This is a good way to mock a function that has to return different values each time it is called, as shown in the following:

```
>>> m = mock.Mock()
>>> m.side_effect = [1, 2, 3]
>>> m()
1
>>> m()
2
>>> m()
3
>>> m()
Traceback (most recent call last):
  File "<stdin>", line 1, in <module>
  File "C:\Python34\lib\unittest\mock.py", line 885, in __call__
    return _mock_self._mock_call(*args, **kwargs)
  File "C:\Python34\lib\unittest\mock.py", line 944, in _mock_call
    result = next(effect)
StopIteration
```

As we have seen, the mocking framework's method of handling side effects using the `side_effect` attribute is very simple, yet quite powerful.

# How much mocking is too much?

In the previous few sections, we've seen the same test written with different levels of mocking. We started off with a test that didn't use any mocks at all, and subsequently mocked out each of the dependencies one by one. Which one of these solutions is the best?

As with many things, this is a point of personal preference. A purist would probably choose to mock out all dependencies. My personal preference is to use real objects when they are small and self-contained. I would not have mocked out the `Stock` class. This is because mocks generally require some configuration with return values or side effects, and this configuration can clutter the test and make it less readable. For small, self-contained classes, it is simpler to just use the real object.

At the other end of the spectrum, classes that might interact with external systems, or that take a lot of memory, or are slow are good candidates for mocking out. Additionally, objects that require a lot of dependencies on other object to initialize are candidates for mocking. With mocks, you just create an object, pass it in, and assert on parts that you are interested in checking. You don't have to create an entirely valid object.

Even here there are alternatives to mocking. For example, when dealing with a database, it is common to mock out the database calls and hardcode a return value into the mock. This is because the database might be on another server, and accessing it makes the tests slow and unreliable. However, instead of mocks, another option could be to use a fast in-memory database for the tests. This allows us to use a live database instead of a mocked out database. Which approach is better depends on the situation.

# Mocks versus stubs versus fakes versus spies

We've been talking about mocks so far, but we've been a little loose on the terminology. Technically, everything we've talked about falls under the category of a **test double**. A test double is some sort of fake object that we use to stand in for a real object in a test case.

Mocks are a specific kind of test double that record information about calls that have been made to it, so that we can assert on them later.

**Stubs** are just an empty do-nothing kind of object or method. They are used when we don't care about some functionality in the test. For example, imagine we have a method that performs a calculation and then sends an e-mail. If we are testing the calculation logic, we might just replace the e-mail sending method with an empty do-nothing method in the test case so that no e-mails are sent out while the test is running.

**Fakes** are a replacement of one object or system with a simpler one that facilitates easier testing. Using an in-memory database instead of the real one, or the way we created a dummy `TestAction` earlier in this chapter would be examples of fakes.

Finally, **spies** are objects that are like middlemen. Like mocks, they record the calls so that we can assert on them later, but after recording, they continue execution to the original code. Spies are different from the other three in the sense that they do not replace any functionality. After recording the call, the real code is still executed. Spies sit in the middle and do not cause any change in execution pattern.

# Patching methods

So far we have looked at simple mocking patterns. These are the methods that you will use most of the time. Python's mocking framework doesn't stop there and has tremendous support for doing more complex things.

Let us look at the `PrintAction` class (put this code in the file `action.py` in the `stock_alerter` directory) as follows:

```
class PrintAction:
    def execute(self, content):
        print(content)
```

This is a simple action, which, when the `execute` method is called, will just print out the alert description to the screen.

Now, how do we go about testing this? What we want to test is that the action actually calls the print method with the right parameters. In the previous examples, we could create a mock object and pass it into the class instead of a real object. Here, there is no parameter or attribute that we can simply replace with a mock object.

The solution to this is to use **patching**. Patching is a way to replace a class or function in the global namespace with a mock version. Because Python allows dynamic access to the globals as well as all imported modules, we can just go in and change which object an identifier points to.

In the following sequence, you can see how we replace the `print` function with another one that takes one parameter and returns the double:

```
>>> # the builtin print function prints a string
>>> print("hello")
hello


>>> # the builtin print function handles multiple parameters
>>> print(1, 2)
1 2


>>> # this is where the print function is mapped
>>> __builtins__.print
<built-in function print>


>>> # make the builtin print point to our own lambda
```

```
>>> __builtins__.print = lambda x: x*2

>>> # calling print now executes our substituted function
>>> print("hello")
'hellohello'

>>> # our lambda does not support two parameters
>>> print(1, 2) Traceback (most recent call last):
  File "<stdin>", line 1, in <module>
TypeError: <lambda>() takes 1 positional argument but 2 were given
```

As we can see above, all calls to `print` now call our own function instead of the default printing implementation.

This gives us the hint we need to proceed with our mocking. What if we just replace the `print` with a mock before running the test? This way the code will end up executing our mock instead of the default print implementation, and we can then assert on the mock that it was called with the right parameters.

The following is an example of this technique:

```
import unittest
from unittest import mock
from ..action import PrintAction


class PrintActionTest(unittest.TestCase):
    def test_executing_action_prints_message(self):
        mock_print = mock.Mock()
        old_print = __builtins__["print"]
        __builtins__["print"] = mock_print
        try:
            action = PrintAction()
            action.execute("GOOG > $10")
            mock_print.assert_called_with("GOOG > $10")
        finally:
            __builtins__["print"] = old_print
```

What's going on here?

1. First, we create the mock function.

2. Next, we save the default print implementation. We need to do this so that we can restore it properly at the end of the test.

3. Finally, we replace the default print with our mock function. Now, every time the print function is called, it will call our mock.

4. We run the test, wrapped around a `try`-`finally` block.

5. In the `finally` block, we restore back the default print implementation.

It is very, very important to restore the default implementation back. Remember, we are changing the global information here, so if we don't restore it back, print will point to our mock function in all the subsequent tests as well. This can lead to some very strange behavior, for example, somewhere else we might expect some output on the screen and nothing is printed, and we end up spending hours trying to figure out why. This is the reason why the test is wrapped in the `try`-`finally` block. This way, the mock gets reset back to the default even if there is an exception thrown in the test.

We just saw how to patch in functions and classes with a mock, and since this is a fairly common task, Python gives us a really nice way to perform patching through the `mock.patch` function.

The `mock.patch` function takes away a lot of the work needed to patch functions. Let us look at a couple of ways to use it.

The first way replicates the way we did our manual patching. We create a patcher and then use the `start` method to execute the patch, and the `stop` method to reset back the original implementation, as shown in the following:

```
def test_executing_action_prints_message(self):
    patcher = mock.patch('builtins.print')
    mock_print = patcher.start()
    try:
        action = PrintAction()
        action.execute("GOOG > $10")
        mock_print.assert_called_with("GOOG > $10")
    finally:
        patcher.stop()
```

Like our manual patching, we have to be careful that the stop method gets called even if an exception is raised.

The patch can also be used as a context manager in conjunction with the `with` keyword. This syntax is a lot cleaner and generally preferable to calling start and stop ourselves:

```
def test_executing_action_prints_message(self):
    with mock.patch('builtins.print') as mock_print:
        action = PrintAction()
        action.execute("GOOG > $10")
        mock_print.assert_called_with("GOOG > $10")
```

Let us walk through what is going on here:

- The code where we want the patch to be active is wrapped inside the `with` block.
- We call the `patch` function, which returns the patcher to be used as a context manager. The mock object is set in the variable specified in the `as` section. In this case, the patched mock is set to `mock_print`.
- Inside the block, we perform the test and assert as usual.
- The patch is removed once execution comes out of the context block. This could be because all the statements were executed or due to an exception.

With this syntax, we don't need to worry about unhandled exceptions causing a problem with the patch.

The `patch` function can also be used as a method decorator, as the following example shows:

```
@mock.patch("builtins.print")
def test_executing_action_prints_message(self, mock_print):
    action = PrintAction()
    action.execute("GOOG > $10")
    mock_print.assert_called_with("GOOG > $10")
```

With this syntax, the patcher patches the required function and passes in the replacement mock object as the first parameter to the test method. We can then use the mock object as normal. The patch is reset once the test completes.

If we need to patch the same object for a number of tests, then we can use the class decorator syntax instead, as shown in the following:

```
@mock.patch("builtins.print")
class PrintActionTest(unittest.TestCase):
    def test_executing_action_prints_message(self, mock_print):
        action = PrintAction()
        action.execute("GOOG > $10")
        mock_print.assert_called_with("GOOG > $10")
```

This syntax decorates all the tests in the class with the patch. By default, the decorator searches for methods that start with test. However, this can be changed by setting the patch.TEST_PREFIX attribute, and the class decorator will patch all methods that start with that prefix.

# An important gotcha when patching

When patching, we should remember to patch exactly the object that the class is using. Python allows multiple references to an object, and it is easy to end up patching the wrong object. We would then spend hours wondering why the mock object isn't being executed.

For example, support file alert.py uses an import like the following:

```
from rule import PriceRule
```

Now in the alert test, if we want to patch out PriceRule, then the following is the way we need to do it:

```
import alert


@mock.patch("alert.PriceRule")
def test_patch_rule(self, mock_rule):
    ....
```

Only if we do it this way will we patch the PriceRule object that is used in alert.py file. The following way will not work:

```
import rule


@mock.patch("rule.PriceRule")
def test_patch_rule(self, mock_rule):
    ....
```

This code will patch out `rule.PriceRule`, which is different from the actual object that we want to patch out. When we run this test, we'll see that the alert executes the real `PriceRule` object and not the one that we patched out.

Since this is such a common mistake, we should check this first if ever we have problems with the test not executing the patched object correctly.

# Tying it all together

Let us tie this chapter together with a more complex example. The following is the code for the `EmailAction` class. This action sends an e-mail to the user when the rule is matched.

```python
import smtplib
from email.mime.text import MIMEText


class EmailAction:
    """Send an email when a rule is matched"""
    from_email = "alerts@stocks.com"

    def __init__(self, to):
        self.to_email = to

    def execute(self, content):
        message = MIMEText(content)
        message["Subject"] = "New Stock Alert"
        message["From"] = "alerts@stocks.com"
        message["To"] = self.to_email
        smtp = smtplib.SMTP("email.stocks.com")
        try:
            smtp.send_message(message)
        finally:
            smtp.quit()
```

The following is how the library works:

1. We instantiate the SMTP class in the smtplib library, passing it the server we want to connect to. This returns the SMTP object.

2. We call the send_message method on the SMTP object, passing in the e-mail message details in the form of a MIMEText object.

3. Finally, we call the quit method. This method always needs to be called, even if there was an exception in sending the message.

Given this, we need to test the following:

1. The right calls are made to the smtplib library, with the right parameters.

2. The message contents (from, to, subject, body) are correct.

3. The quit method is called even if an exception was thrown when sending the message.

Let us start with a simple test. This test is for verifying that the SMTP class is initialized with the right parameters:

```
class EmailActionTest(unittest.TestCase):
    def setUp(self):
        self.action =
            EmailAction(to="siddharta@silverstripesoftware.com")


    def test_email_is_sent_to_the_right_server(self,
        mock_smtp_class):
        self.action.execute("MSFT has crossed $10 price level")
        mock_smtp_class.assert_called_with("email.stocks.com")
```

First, we start out by patching out the SMTP class in the smtplib module. Since we'll be doing this for every test, we set this up as a class decorator. We then instantiate the EmailAction that we want to test in the setUp.

The test itself is fairly simple. We call the execute method of the action and assert that the mock class was instantiated with the right parameter.

The following test verifies that the right calls are made to SMTP object:

```
    def test_connection_closed_after_sending_mail(self, mock_smtp_class):
        mock_smtp = mock_smtp_class.return_value
        self.action.execute("MSFT has crossed $10 price level")
        mock_smtp.send_message.assert_called_with(mock.ANY)
        self.assertTrue(mock_smtp.quit.called)
```

```
mock_smtp.assert_has_calls([
    mock.call.send_message(mock.ANY),
    mock.call.quit()])
```

There are a few new approaches in this test that are worth discussing.

First is the subtle difference in this series of tests where we are mocking the SMTP class and not an *object*. In the first test, we were checking the parameters passed to the constructor. Since we mocked the class, we could assert directly on our mock object.

In this test, we need to check that the right calls are made on the SMTP *object*. Since an object is the return value from initializing the class, we can access the mock smtp object from the return value of the mock smtp class. This is exactly what we are doing in the first line of the test.

Next, we execute the action as usual.

Finally, we are using the assert_has_calls method to assert that the right calls were made. We could have asserted the calls like the following instead:

```
mock_smtp.send_message.assert_called_with(mock.ANY)
self.assertTrue(mock_smtp.quit.called)
```

The main difference is that the above assertions do not assert the sequence. Suppose the action calls the quit method first and then calls send_message, it would still pass these two assertions. However, the assert_has_calls assertion not only checks that the methods were called, but also checks that the quit method is called after send_message.

The following third test checks that the connection is closed even if an exception is raised when sending the message:

```
def test_connection_closed_if_send_gives_error(self,
    mock_smtp_class):
    mock_smtp = mock_smtp_class.return_value
    mock_smtp.send_message.side_effect =
    smtplib.SMTPServerDisconnected()
    try:
        self.action.execute("MSFT has crossed $10 price level")
    except Exception:
        pass
    self.assertTrue(mock_smtp.quit.called)
```

In this test, we use the `side_effect` attribute to set the send message mock to raise an exception. We then check that the `quit` method was called even when the exception was raised.

In the last test, we need to check that the right message contents are passed to `send_message`. The function takes a `MIMEText` object as a parameter. How do we check that the right object was passed?

The following is one way that *does not* work:

```
def test_email_is_sent_with_the_right_subject(self, mock_smtp_class):
    mock_smtp = mock_smtp_class.return_value
    self.action.execute("MSFT has crossed $10 price level")
    message = MIMEText("MSFT has crossed $10 price level")
    message["Subject"] = "New Stock Alert"
    message["From"] = "alerts@stocks.com"
    message["To"] = "siddharta@silverstripesoftware.com"
    mock_smtp.send_message.assert_called_with(message)
```

If we run the above test, we'll get a failure like the following:

```
AssertionError: Expected call: send_message(<email.mime.text.MIMEText
object at 0x0000000003641F98>)
Actual call: send_message(<email.mime.text.MIMEText object at
0x000000000363A0F0>)
```

The problem is that although the contents of the expected `MIMEText` object and the actual one passed to `send_message` are the same, the test still fails because they are both different objects. The mocking framework compares the two parameters by equality, and since both are two different objects, the test for equality fails.

One approach around this problem is to go into the mock, extract the arguments that were passed in the call, and check that they contained the right data. The following is a test that uses this approach:

```
def test_email_is_sent_with_the_right_subject(self, mock_smtp_class):
    mock_smtp = mock_smtp_class.return_value
    self.action.execute("MSFT has crossed $10 price level")
    call_args, _ = mock_smtp.send_message.call_args
    sent_message = call_args[0]
    self.assertEqual("New Stock Alert", sent_message["Subject"])
```

Once the `execute` method is called, we then access the `call_args` attribute of the `mock` object to get the arguments that were passed to `send_message`. We take the first parameter, which is the `MIMEText` object that we are interested in. We then assert that the subject was as expected.

A more elegant way is possible. Remember we said that the mocking framework compares parameters by equality? This means that we can pass in an object that implements the __eq__ special method and use that to perform any comparison that we want. The following is one such class for checking equality between two `MIMEText` messages:

```
class MessageMatcher:
    def __init__(self, expected):
        self.expected = expected


    def __eq__(self, other):
        return self.expected["Subject"] == other["Subject"] and \
            self.expected["From"] == other["From"] and \
            self.expected["To"] == other["To"] and \
            self.expected["Message"] == other._payload
```

This class basically takes a dictionary of values, and then can be used to compare whether a `MIMEText` object contains those values (at least the values we are interested in). Since it implements the __eq__ method, a direct equality can be used to check, as shown in the following:

```
>>> message = MIMEText("d")
>>> message["Subject"] = "a"
>>> message["From"] = "b"
>>> message["To"] = "c"
>>> expected = MessageMatcher({"Subject":"a", "From":"b", "To":"c",
"Message":"d"})
>>> message == expected
True
```

We can use this technique to pass in such an object as the expected parameter of a test like the following:

```
def test_email_is_sent_when_action_is_executed(self,
    mock_smtp_class):
    expected_message = {
        "Subject": "New Stock Alert",
```

```
        "Message": "MSFT has crossed $10 price level",
        "To": "siddharta@silverstripesoftware.com",
        "From": "alerts@stocks.com"
    }
    mock smtp = mock_smtp_class.return_value
    self.action.execute("MSFT has crossed $10 price level")
    mock_smtp.send_message.assert_called_with(
        MessageMatcher(expected_message))
```

Writing custom parameter matchers like this is an easy way to assert on parameters for which we might not have direct object access, or when we want to compare only a few attributes of the object for the purposes of the test.

# Summary

In this chapter, you looked at how to use mocks to test interactions between objects. You saw how to hand write our own mocks, followed by using the mocking framework provided in the Python standard library. Next, you saw how to use patching for more advanced mocking. We wrapped it up by looking at a slightly more complex mocking example that had us put all the mocking techniques into practice.

So far you have been looking at writing tests for new code. In the next chapter, you will take a look at how to deal with existing code that does not have tests.

# 5
# Working with Legacy Code

Having a solid set of unit tests is critical for a successful project. As you have seen so far, not only do unit tests help prevent bugs from getting into the code, but they also help in many other ways such as guiding the design, enabling us to refactor the code and keep it more maintainable, as well as a reference where you can see what the expected behavior is supposed to be.

TDD is the best way to ensure that our code has all the properties mentioned in the preceding paragraph. But, as anyone who has worked on larger, more complex projects knows, there are always pieces of code that don't have tests. Usually, this is the code written many years ago, long before we started practicing TDD. Or, it might have been the code that was written in a hurry to meet an urgent deadline.

Either way, this is the code that does not have associated tests. The code is often messy. It has a ton of dependencies on other classes. And now, we need to add a new feature to this code. How do we approach this? Should we just go in there and hack in our new feature? Or is there a better way?

## What is legacy code?

In this chapter, we will use the term **legacy code** to mean any code that does not have unit tests. This is a rather broad definition, since it includes the code that was written long ago as well as recent code, which, for some reason, was written without tests. Although not strictly about the old code, this is a popular definition in the TDD community, made mainstream by Michael Feathers' excellent book *Working Effectively with Legacy Code* (Prentice Hall, 2004), and this is the meaning we will adopt in this book as well.

There are five steps to working with the legacy code:

1.  **Understanding the code**: If we are lucky, we will have some great documentation that will help us understand the code that we are going to touch. More likely, documentation will be scant or not present altogether. Since there are no tests, we cannot read the tests to try to understand what the code is supposed to do. And for really old code, chances are that the person who wrote the code does not work for your organization anymore. It sounds like the perfect storm to mess with us, but as anyone who has worked on large production projects can attest, this is the norm for the majority of the codebase. So, our first step is to just understand the code and figure out what is going on.

2.  **Breaking dependencies**: Once we start to understand the code, our next step would be to write some tests for the code. This is not straightforward for the legacy code because the design is often a spaghetti mess of dependencies with other files and classes. We need some way to break these dependencies before we can write unit tests.

3.  **Writing tests**: We are now finally in a position to write some unit tests for the code we are about to modify.

4.  **Refactoring**: Now that we have tests, we can start applying some of the refactoring techniques that we saw earlier in this book.

5.  **Implementing the new feature**: Having cleaned up the code, we can now implement the new feature, with tests, of course.

Although the preceding steps are shown as a linear sequence, it is important to understand that the steps often take place in a non-linear way. For example, while trying to understand a large method, we might take a small piece of code, extract it to a method, look at it in greater detail, and then write a couple of tests for it, finally going back to the original method and looking at another piece of the method. We might then come back to our extracted methods and extract them into a new class. The steps go back and forth until we are in a position to safely implement the new feature without the risk of breaking stuff.

# Understanding the code

The following is the code that we are going to be looking at in this chapter:

```
from datetime import datetime


from .stock import Stock
```

```
from .rule import PriceRule


class AlertProcessor:
    def __init__(self):
        self.exchange = {"GOOG": Stock("GOOG"),
            "AAPL": Stock("AAPL")}
        rule_1 = PriceRule("GOOG", lambda stock: stock.price > 10)
        rule_2 = PriceRule("AAPL", lambda stock: stock.price > 5)
        self.exchange["GOOG"].updated.connect(
            lambda stock: print(stock.symbol, stock.price) \
                if rule_1.matches(self.exchange) else None)
        self.exchange["AAPL"].updated.connect(
            lambda stock: print(stock.symbol, stock.price) \
                if rule_2.matches(self.exchange) else None)


        updates = []
        with open("updates.csv", "r") as fp:
            for line in fp.readlines():
                symbol, timestamp, price = line.split(",")
                updates.append((symbol, datetime.strptime(timestamp,
                    "%Y-%m-%dT%H:%M:%S.%f"), int(price)))


        for symbol, timestamp, price in updates:
            stock = self.exchange[symbol]
            stock.update(timestamp, price)
```

This is a piece of code that does something. All we know is that it takes some updates from a file and runs it through some alerts. The following is what the updates.csv file looks like:

```
GOOG,2014-02-11T14:10:22.13,5
AAPL,2014-02-11T00:00:00.0,8
GOOG,2014-02-11T14:11:22.13,3
GOOG,2014-02-11T14:12:22.13,15
AAPL,2014-02-11T00:00:00.0,10
GOOG,2014-02-11T14:15:22.13,21
```

We now need to add a few features to this code:

- We need to be able to get updates from a network server
- We need to be able to send an e-mail when an alert is matched

Before we can get started, we need to be able to understand the current code. We do this by characterization tests.

# What are characterization tests?

**Characterization tests** are tests that describe the current behavior of the code. We aren't writing the tests against a predefined expectation. Instead, we write the tests against the actual behavior. You may ask what this accomplishes since the test can't fail if we are going to look at the current behavior and write a test that looks for the same thing. However, the thing to remember is that we aren't trying to find bugs. Instead, by writing tests against the current behavior, we are building up a safety net of tests. If we break something during the process of refactoring, the test will fail and we will know that we have to undo our changes.

# Using the Python interactive shell to understand the code

So what does this piece of code do? Let's open up the Python interactive shell and take a look. The interactive shell is a great help because it allows us to play around with the code, trying different input values and seeing what kind of output we get. Let's open the class now as follows:

```
>>> from stock_alerter.legacy import AlertProcessor
>>> processor = AlertProcessor()
AAPL 8
GOOG 15
AAPL 10
GOOG 21
>>>
```

As we can see, just instantiating the class has caused the code to run and we have some output printed on the terminal. This is not surprising given that all the code is within the __init__ method.

# Writing a characterization test

Okay, we now have something to write a test for. We understand that when the input in the `updates.csv` file is as follows:

```
GOOG,2014-02-11T14:10:22.13,5
AAPL,2014-02-11T00:00:00.0,8
GOOG,2014-02-11T14:11:22.13,3
GOOG,2014-02-11T14:12:22.13,15
AAPL,2014-02-11T00:00:00.0,10
GOOG,2014-02-11T14:15:22.13,21
```

Then, the output when we instantiate the class is as follows:

```
AAPL 8
GOOG 15
AAPL 10
GOOG 21
```

We may not yet know why this is the output or how it was calculated, but this is enough to get started with a test. The following is what the test looks like:

```python
import unittest
from unittest import mock

from ..legacy import AlertProcessor

class AlertProcessorTest(unittest.TestCase):
    @mock.patch("builtins.print")
    def test_processor_characterization_1(self, mock_print):
        AlertProcessor()
        mock_print.assert_has_calls([mock.call("AAPL", 8),
                                     mock.call("GOOG", 15),
                                     mock.call("AAPL", 10),
                                     mock.call("GOOG", 21)])
```

All this test does is to mock out the `print` function and then instantiate the class. We assert that the required data is printed out.

Is this a great unit test? Probably not. For one, it still takes the input from the `updates.csv` file. Ideally, we would have mocked out the file access. But it doesn't matter at the moment. This test passes and it will be a safety net when we start modifying the code. That is all we need the test to do for now.

# Using pdb to understand the code

The Python interactive shell is a great way to understand the code at the boundaries of method calls. It allows us to pass in various combinations of input and see what kind of output we get. But what if we want to see what is going on within a function or method? This is where `pdb` can be extremely useful.

**pdb** is a Python Debugger, and it supplies as a part of the Python standard library. It has a number of features such as being able to step through the execution line by line, see how variables change, and set and remove breakpoints. pdb is very powerful, and there are a number of good books that cover it in detail. We won't go through all the features in this book, but just give a short example of how it can be used to understand the code.

To execute the code from within `pdb`, run the following lines in the interactive shell:

```
>>> import pdb
>>> from stock_alerter.legacy import AlertProcessor
>>> pdb.run("AlertProcessor()")
> <string>(1)<module>()
(Pdb)
```

The `pdb.run` method allows us to specify any string as a parameter. That string is executed within the debugger. In this case, we are instantiating the class that starts executing all the code.

At this point, we get the `(Pdb)` prompt from where we can walk through the execution, line by line. You can get help on the various commands available by typing `help`, as shown in the following:

```
(Pdb) help

Documented commands (type help <topic>):
EOF     c         d         h         list      q          rv
undisplay
a       cl        debug     help      ll        quit       s          unt
alias   clear     disable   ignore    longlist  r          source     until
args    commands  display   interact  n         restart    step       up
```

| b | condition | down | j | next | return | tbreak | w |
|---|---|---|---|---|---|---|---|
| break | cont | enable | jump | p | retval | u | whatis |
| bt | continue | exit | l | pp | run | unalias | where |

Miscellaneous help topics:

pdb   exec

(Pdb)

Or, you can also get help by typing `help <command>` for help on a specific command:

```
(Pdb) help s
s(tep)
        Execute the current line, stop at the first possible occasion
        (either in a function that is called or in the current
        function).
(Pdb)
```

# Some common pdb commands

Most of the time, we will use the following commands:

- s: This executes one line of code (going inside a function call if required)
- n: This executes code until you reach the next line in the current function
- r: This executes code until the current function returns
- q: This quits the debugger
- b: This sets a breakpoint on a particular line of a file
- cl: This clears breakpoints
- c: This continues execution until a breakpoint is encountered or until the end of execution

These commands should be enough to move around code and try to inspect what is going on. pdb has a ton of other commands that we won't cover here.

# Walking through a pdb session

Let's now put this into practice. The following is a walk-through of our code using pdb.

First, we run our command within pdb as follows:

```
>>> import pdb
>>> from stock_alerter.legacy import AlertProcessor
>>> pdb.run("AlertProcessor()")
> <string>(1)<module>()
(Pdb)
```

Let's step into the first line as follows:

```
(Pdb) s
--Call--
> c:\projects\tdd_with_python\src\stock_alerter\legacy.py(8)__init__()
-> def __init__(self):
(Pdb)
```

pdb tells us that we are now within the __init__ method. The n command will take us through the first few lines of this method, as shown in the following:

```
(Pdb) n
> c:\projects\tdd_with_python\src\stock_alerter\legacy.py(9)__init__()
-> self.exchange = {"GOOG": Stock("GOOG"), "AAPL": Stock("AAPL")}
(Pdb) n
> c:\projects\tdd_with_python\src\stock_alerter\legacy.py(10)__init__()
-> rule_1 = PriceRule("GOOG", lambda stock: stock.price > 10)
(Pdb) n
> c:\projects\tdd_with_python\src\stock_alerter\legacy.py(11)__init__()
-> rule_2 = PriceRule("AAPL", lambda stock: stock.price > 5)
(Pdb) n
> c:\projects\tdd_with_python\src\stock_alerter\legacy.py(12)__init__()
-> self.exchange["GOOG"].updated.connect(
(Pdb) n
> c:\projects\tdd_with_python\src\stock_alerter\legacy.py(13)__init__()
-> lambda stock: print(stock.symbol, stock.price) \
(Pdb) n
> c:\projects\tdd_with_python\src\stock_alerter\legacy.py(15)__init__()
```

```
-> self.exchange["AAPL"].updated.connect(
(Pdb) n
> c:\projects\tdd_with_python\src\stock_alerter\legacy.py(16)__init__()
-> lambda stock: print(stock.symbol, stock.price) \
(Pdb) n
> c:\projects\tdd_with_python\src\stock_alerter\legacy.py(18)__init__()
-> updates = []
(Pdb)
```

We can examine the initialization that seems to have been done by looking at some of the variables as follows:

```
(Pdb) self.exchange
{'GOOG': <stock_alerter.stock.Stock object at 0x0000000002E59400>,
 'AAPL': <stock_alerter.stock.Stock object at 0x0000000002E593C8>}
(Pdb) rule_1
<stock_alerter.rule.PriceRule object at 0x0000000002E205F8>
```

We can even try executing some of the local variables with various input as follows:

```
(Pdb) test_stock = Stock("GOOG")
(Pdb) test_stock.update(datetime.now(), 100)
(Pdb) rule_1.matches({"GOOG": test_stock})
True
(Pdb)
```

This helps us understand the state of various objects during different parts of execution.

The next section of code is the part where we open the file and read it. Let's skip ahead of this by putting a breakpoint on line 25 and executing right to it with the c command, as shown in the following:

```
(Pdb) b stock_alerter\legacy.py:25
Breakpoint 1 at c:\projects\tdd_with_python\src\stock_alerter\legacy.py:25
(Pdb) c
> c:\projects\tdd_with_python\src\stock_alerter\legacy.py(25)__init__()
-> for symbol, timestamp, price in updates:
(Pdb)
```

Now that the file reading part is done, we can inspect the format of data that was read by examining the updates local variable. The pp command does a pretty print so that the output is easier to read, as shown in the following:

```
(Pdb) pp updates
[('GOOG', datetime.datetime(2014, 2, 11, 14, 10, 22, 130000), 5),
 ('AAPL', datetime.datetime(2014, 2, 11, 0, 0), 8),
 ('GOOG', datetime.datetime(2014, 2, 11, 14, 11, 22, 130000), 3),
 ('GOOG', datetime.datetime(2014, 2, 11, 14, 12, 22, 130000), 15),
 ('AAPL', datetime.datetime(2014, 2, 11, 0, 0), 10),
 ('GOOG', datetime.datetime(2014, 2, 11, 14, 15, 22, 130000), 21)]
```

Looks like the file got parsed into a list of tuples, each containing (stock symbol, timestamp, price). Let's see what would happen if we had only the GOOG updates, as shown in the following:

```
(Pdb) updates = [update for update in updates if update[0] == "GOOG"]
(Pdb) pp updates
[('GOOG', datetime.datetime(2014, 2, 11, 14, 10, 22, 130000), 5),
 ('GOOG', datetime.datetime(2014, 2, 11, 14, 11, 22, 130000), 3),
 ('GOOG', datetime.datetime(2014, 2, 11, 14, 12, 22, 130000), 15),
 ('GOOG', datetime.datetime(2014, 2, 11, 14, 15, 22, 130000), 21)]
```

There we go. As we can see, it is even possible to change the values held by local variables midway during execution. The following is the output when we run the remainder of the code:

```
(Pdb) cl
Clear all breaks? y
Deleted breakpoint 4 at c:\projects\tdd_with_python\src\stock_alerter\
legacy.py:25
(Pdb) c
GOOG 15
GOOG 21
>>>
```

The cl command clears the breakpoint, and we use the c command to run to the end of the execution. The output with the modified the updates variable gets printed. Since the execution is complete at this point, we are returned back to the interactive shell.

Our exploration is done for now. At any point, we could have quit the debugger as follows:

```
(Pdb) q
>>>
```

Quitting the debugger takes us back to the interactive shell. At this point, we might add a few more characterization tests based on the exploration that we just did.

# Techniques to break dependencies

Now that we've seen some techniques to help us understand the code, our next step is to break dependencies. This will help us write further characterization tests. To do this, we will *very carefully* start modifying the code. All the while, we will try to stick to the following goals:

- Make small changes that are very unlikely to break
- Try to change the public interface as little as possible

Why these goals? Because we have a lack of tests, we have to be careful with the changes we make. Hence, small changes are better. We also need to be careful of changing the public interface because we have to go and fix all the other files and modules that use this class.

# The Rope refactoring library

The **Rope refactoring library** is a library to perform automated refactoring of your code. For example, you could select a few lines and then type the command to extract it into a method. The library will automatically create this method with the appropriate code, parameters, and return value, and will automatically place a call to the newly extracted method in place of the original code. Automated refactoring in Python is a little tricky because the dynamic nature of the language makes it difficult to identify all the changes correctly. However, it is ideal for making small changes, like we are going to do in this chapter.

Since it is a library, Rope doesn't have any UI for performing the refactorings. Instead, it is integrated into the development environment, as either an IDE or a text editor. Most popular IDEs and text editors have support for integrating with Rope. Rope is available at https://github.com/python-rope/rope.

If your IDE or text editor of choice supports integration with Rope, or has built-in refactoring capabilities, then use it as far as possible.

# Separate initialization from execution

One of the problems that the class we are working with has is that the whole execution happens in the __init__ method. This means that as soon as the class is constructed, everything is executed before we have a change to set up mocks or make other changes that will help us write characterization tests. Luckily, there is a simple solution to this. We will simply move the execution part into a separate method as follows:

```python
class AlertProcessor:
    def __init__(self):
        self.exchange = {"GOOG": Stock("GOOG"), "AAPL":
            Stock("AAPL")}
        rule_1 = PriceRule("GOOG", lambda stock: stock.price > 10)
        rule_2 = PriceRule("AAPL", lambda stock: stock.price > 5)
        self.exchange["GOOG"].updated.connect(
            lambda stock: print(stock.symbol, stock.price) \
                    if rule_1.matches(self.exchange) else None)
        self.exchange["AAPL"].updated.connect(
            lambda stock: print(stock.symbol, stock.price) \
                    if rule_2.matches(self.exchange) else None)

    def run(self):
        updates = []
        with open("updates.csv", "r") as fp:
            for line in fp.readlines():
                symbol, timestamp, price = line.split(",")
                updates.append(
                    (symbol,
                    datetime.strptime(timestamp,
                            "%Y-%m-%dT%H:%M:%S.%f"),
                    int(price)))

        for symbol, timestamp, price in updates:
            stock = self.exchange[symbol]
            stock.update(timestamp, price)
```

The astute reader would have observed that we have just broken our second goal—to minimize changes to the public interface. The change that we've made has changed the interface. If there are other modules using this class, they would have only constructed the class, assuming all the processing is complete. We have to now go and find all the places where we are creating this class and add a call to the run method. Otherwise, the class will not work as expected.

To prevent having to fix all the callers, we can call the run method ourselves from within the initializer like the following:

```
def __init__(self):
    self.exchange = {"GOOG": Stock("GOOG"), "AAPL": Stock("AAPL")}
    rule_1 = PriceRule("GOOG", lambda stock: stock.price > 10)
    rule_2 = PriceRule("AAPL", lambda stock: stock.price > 5)
    self.exchange["GOOG"].updated.connect(
        lambda stock: print(stock.symbol, stock.price) \
                    if rule_1.matches(self.exchange) else None)
    self.exchange["AAPL"].updated.connect(
        lambda stock: print(stock.symbol, stock.price) \
                    if rule_2.matches(self.exchange) else None)
    self.run()
```

All the tests pass again, but once again, all the codes get executed the moment we instantiate the class. Are we back to square one? Let's see in the next section.

# Use default values for parameters

One of the most useful features of Python is the concept of being able to set a default value for a parameter. This allows us to change the interface, while making it look just the same for existing callers.

In the previous section, we moved a piece of code into the run method, and we called this method from the __init__ method. It seems like we haven't really changed anything, but that is misleading.

Here is the next change to the __init__ method:

```
def __init__(self, autorun=True):
    self.exchange = {"GOOG": Stock("GOOG"), "AAPL": Stock("AAPL")}
    rule_1 = PriceRule("GOOG", lambda stock: stock.price > 10)
    rule_2 = PriceRule("AAPL", lambda stock: stock.price > 5)
    self.exchange["GOOG"].updated.connect(
```

```
        lambda stock: print(stock.symbol, stock.price) \
                    if rule_1.matches(self.exchange) else None)
    self.exchange["AAPL"].updated.connect(
        lambda stock: print(stock.symbol, stock.price) \
                    if rule_2.matches(sclf.exchange) else None)
if autorun:
    self.run()
```

What we have done is to introduce a new parameter called autorun and set the default value as True. We then wrap the call to the run method with a conditional. Only if autorun is True will the run method be called.

All the existing callers who use this class will be unchanged—when the constructor is called without parameters, the autorun parameter will be set to True and the run method will be called. Everything will be as expected.

But adding the parameter gives us the option to explicitly set the autorun parameter to False in our tests, and thus avoid the run method from being called. We can now instantiate the class, then set up any mocks or other test initialization that we want, and then proceed to manually call the run method in the test.

The following is the same characterization test that we wrote earlier, rewritten to take advantage of this new functionality:

```
def test_processor_characterization_2(self):
    processor = AlertProcessor(autorun=False)
    with mock.patch("builtins.print") as mock_print:
        processor.run()
    mock_print.assert_has_calls([mock.call("AAPL", 8),
                                 mock.call("GOOG", 15),
                                 mock.call("AAPL", 10),
                                 mock.call("GOOG", 21)])
```

Bingo! That one change seems small now, but it is the change that enables us to write all the characterization tests that follow.

# Extract the method and test

It is very difficult to test methods that are large. This is because tests can only check inputs, outputs, and interactions. It becomes a problem if there are just a couple of lines within the whole method that we want to test.

Let's take a look at the `run` method again, as shown in the following:

```python
def run(self):
    updates = []
    with open("updates.csv", "r") as fp:
        for line in fp.readlines():
            symbol, timestamp, price = line.split(",")
            updates.append((symbol, datetime.strptime(timestamp,
                "%Y-%m-%dT%H:%M:%S.%f"), int(price)))


    for symbol, timestamp, price in updates:
        stock = self.exchange[symbol]
        stock.update(timestamp, price)
```

Suppose we want to just write characterization tests for the code in the second loop.
How can do that? A simple way is to extract those lines into a separate method, as
shown in the following:

```python
def do_updates(self, updates):
    for symbol, timestamp, price in updates:
        stock = self.exchange[symbol]
        stock.update(timestamp, price)
```

And we need to call the new method in the original place, as shown in the following:

```python
def run(self):
    updates = []
    with open("updates.csv", "r") as fp:
        for line in fp.readlines():
            symbol, timestamp, price = line.split(",")
            updates.append((symbol, datetime.strptime(timestamp,
                "%Y-%m-%dT%H:%M:%S.%f"), int(price)))
    self.do_updates(updates)
```

We can now write characterization tests for this new method as follows:

```python
def test_processor_characterization_3(self):
    processor = AlertProcessor(autorun=False)
    mock_goog = mock.Mock()
    processor.exchange = {"GOOG": mock_goog}
```

```
updates = [("GOOG", datetime(2014, 12, 8), 5)]
processor.do_updates(updates)
mock_goog.update.assert_called_with(datetime(2014, 12, 8), 5)
```

Ideally, we try to extract small groups of code so that the Extract Method refactoring is easy to perform without mistakes. Remember, we don't have the safety net of existing unit test here.

# Inject dependencies

In the previous characterization test, we instantiated the class and then proceeded to replace the exchange instance variable with another one in which the Stock class was mocked out. Another way of achieving this aim is to use the earlier trick of introducing default variables like the following:

```
def __init__(self, autorun=True, exchange=None):
    if exchange is None:
        self.exchange = {"GOOG": Stock("GOOG"), "AAPL":
            Stock("AAPL")}
    else:
        self.exchange = exchange
    rule_1 = PriceRule("GOOG", lambda stock: stock.price > 10)
    rule_2 = PriceRule("AAPL", lambda stock: stock.price > 5)
    self.exchange["GOOG"].updated.connect(
        lambda stock: print(stock.symbol, stock.price) \
            if rule_1.matches(self.exchange) else None)
    self.exchange["AAPL"].updated.connect(
        lambda stock: print(stock.symbol, stock.price) \
            if rule_2.matches(self.exchange) else None)
    if autorun:
        self.run()
```

This allows us to inject in a mock when writing the characterization test, as shown in the following:

```
def test_processor_characterization_4(self):
    mock_goog = mock.Mock()
    mock_aapl = mock.Mock()
    exchange = {"GOOG": mock_goog, "AAPL": mock_aapl}
    processor = AlertProcessor(autorun=False, exchange=exchange)
```

```
updates = [("GOOG", datetime(2014, 12, 8), 5)]
processor.do_updates(updates)
mock_goog.update.assert_called_with(datetime(2014, 12, 8), 5)
```

# Inherit and test

Another way to achieve this goal is by writing a class that inherits from `AlertProcessor`, but includes parameters for the dependencies.

For example, we could create a class like the following in the test file:

```
class TestAlertProcessor(AlertProcessor):
    def __init__(self, exchange):
        AlertProcessor.__init__(self, autorun=False)
        self.exchange = exchange
```

This class inherits from `AlertProcessor` and takes in the parameters that we want to mock out in our characterization tests. The `__init__` method calls the original class initializer and then overrides the `exchange` parameter with the value passed to it.

In the unit test, we can instantiate the test class instead of the real one. We pass in an exchange that contains mock stock objects. The mocks get set, and we can test that the right calls were made, as shown in the following:

```
def test_processor_characterization_5(self):
    mock_goog = mock.Mock()
    mock_aapl = mock.Mock()
    exchange = {"GOOG": mock_goog, "AAPL": mock_aapl}
    processor = TestAlertProcessor(exchange)
    updates = [("GOOG", datetime(2014, 12, 8), 5)]
    processor.do_updates(updates)
    mock_goog.update.assert_called_with(datetime(2014, 12, 8), 5)
```

The advantage of this method compared to injecting dependencies via default parameters is that it does not require changing any code in the original class.

# Stubbing local methods

Most of the time, we use mocks to double for other classes or functions apart from the class being tested. For example, we mocked out the `Stock` objects in the example from the previous section, and we mocked out the `print` built-in function earlier in the chapter.

However, Python does not stop us from mocking out methods of the same class that we are testing. This is a powerful way of testing complex classes.

Let's say that we want to test the code in the `run` method that parses the file, without executing the part that updates the stock values. The following is a test that does just that:

```
def test_processor_characterization_6(self):
    processor = AlertProcessor(autorun=False)
    processor.do_updates = mock.Mock()
    processor.run()
    processor.do_updates.assert_called_with([
        ('GOOG', datetime(2014, 2, 11, 14, 10, 22, 130000), 5),
        ('AAPL', datetime(2014, 2, 11, 0, 0), 8),
        ('GOOG', datetime(2014, 2, 11, 14, 11, 22, 130000), 3),
        ('GOOG', datetime(2014, 2, 11, 14, 12, 22, 130000), 15),
        ('AAPL', datetime(2014, 2, 11, 0, 0), 10),
        ('GOOG', datetime(2014, 2, 11, 14, 15, 22, 130000), 21)])
```

In the test above, we stub out the `do_updates` method of the class before executing the `run` method. When we execute `run`, it parses the file, then instead of running the `do_updates` local method, it executes our mocked out method instead. Since the real method is stubbed out, the code does not update the `Stock` or print anything to the screen. All that functionality has been stubbed out. We then test whether the parsing was correct by checking whether the right parameters were passed to the `do_updates` method.

Stubbing out a local method is a good way to understand a more complex class because it allows us to write characterization tests for small parts of the class in isolation.

# Extract the method and stub

Sometimes, a method is quite long and we want to stub out a part of the method. We can combine the above techniques by extracting the part we want to stub out into a local method, and then stub out the method in the test.

The following is what our `run` method currently looks like:

```
def run(self):
    updates = []
    with open("updates.csv", "r") as fp:
        for line in fp.readlines():
            symbol, timestamp, price = line.split(",")
            updates.append((symbol, datetime.strptime(timestamp,
                "%Y-%m-%dT%H:%M:%S.%f"), int(price)))
    self.do_updates(updates)
```

Let's say that we want the tests to skip the part of the method where the file is read and parsed.

We first extract the lines into a method as follows:

```
def parse_file(self):
    updates = []
    with open("updates.csv", "r") as fp:
        for line in fp.readlines():
            symbol, timestamp, price = line.split(",")
            updates.append((symbol, datetime.strptime(timestamp,
                "%Y-%m-%dT%H:%M:%S.%f"), int(price)))
    return updates
```

Then, we replace the lines in the `run` method with a call to the newly extracted method as follows:

```
def run(self):
    updates = self.parse_file()
    self.do_updates(updates)
```

Finally, the characterization test mocks out the newly extracted method, gives it a return value, and calls the `run` method, as shown in the following:

```
def test_processor_characterization_7(self):
    processor = AlertProcessor(autorun=False)
    processor.parse_file = mock.Mock()
```

```
processor.parse_file.return_value = [
    ('GOOG', datetime(2014, 2, 11, 14, 12, 22, 130000), 15)]
with mock.patch("builtins.print") as mock_print:
    processor.run()
mock_print.assert called_with("GOOG", 15)
```

With the file parsing lines extracted into a separate method, we can easily write a number of different characterization tests for different combinations of inputs. For example, the following is another characterization test that checks nothing is printed to screen for a different input:

```
def test_processor_characterization_8(self):
    processor = AlertProcessor(autorun=False)
    processor.parse_file = mock.Mock()
    processor.parse_file.return_value = [
        ('GOOG', datetime(2014, 2, 11, 14, 10, 22, 130000), 5)]
    with mock.patch("builtins.print") as mock_print:
        processor.run()
    self.assertFalse(mock_print.called)
```

We can also use this technique to test hard to access code such as `lambda` functions. We extract the `lambda` function into a separate function, which enables us to write characterization tests for it separately or mock it when writing tests for other parts of the code.

Let's do the following for our code. First, extract the `lambda` function to a local method.

```
def print_action(self, stock, rule):
    print(stock.symbol, stock.price) \
        if rule.matches(self.exchange) else None
```

Then, replace the `print` lines with a call to the method as follows:

```
self.exchange["GOOG"].updated.connect(
    lambda stock: self.print_action(stock, rule_1))
self.exchange["AAPL"].updated.connect(
    lambda stock: self.print_action(stock, rule_2))
```

 Notice how we have made the call. We still use a lambda function, but delegate to the local method with the appropriate parameters.

We can now mock out this method when writing the characterization tests for the
`do_updates` method:

```
def test_processor_characterization_9(self):
    processor = AlertProcessor(autorun=False)
    processor.print_action = mock.Mock()
    processor.do_updates([
        ('GOOG', datetime(2014, 2, 11, 14, 12, 22, 130000), 15)])
    self.assertTrue(processor.print_action.called)
```

# The cycle continues

All the techniques mentioned in the last section help us isolate pieces of code and
break dependencies with other classes. This allows us to introduce stubs and mocks,
making it easier to write more detailed characterization tests. The Extract Method
refactoring is used a lot and is a great technique to isolate small sections of code.

The whole process is iterative. In a typical session, we might look at a piece of code
via `pdb`, and then decide to extract it to a method. We might then experiment with
passing different inputs to the extracted method in the interactive shell, following
which we might write a few characterization tests. We would then go back to another
section of the class and write more tests after mocking or stubbing the new method,
following which we might go back into `pdb` or the interactive shell to take a look at
another piece of code.

Throughout the process, we keep making small changes that are unlikely to break
and keep running all our existing characterization tests to test that we haven't
broken anything.

# Time to refactor

After a while, we might end up with a pretty good suite of characterization tests
for the legacy code. We can now approach this code like any other well-tested code
and start applying the bigger refactorings with an aim to improve the design before
adding our new features.

For example, we might decide to extract the `print_action` method into a separate
`Action` class, or the `parse_file` method into a `Reader` class.

The following is a `FileReader` class where we have moved the contents from the `parse_file` local method:

```python
class FileReader:
    def __init__(self, filename):
        self.filename = filcname

    def get_updates(self):
        updates = []
        with open("updates.csv", "r") as fp:
            for line in fp.readlines():
                symbol, timestamp, price = line.split(",")
                updates.append((symbol,
                    datetime.strptime(timestamp,
                    "%Y-%m-%dT%H:%M:%S.%f"), int(price)))
        return updates
```

We then use the Inject Dependencies pattern to pass the `reader` as a parameter to the constructor:

```python
def __init__(self, autorun=True, reader=None, exchange=None):
    self.reader = reader if reader else FileReader("updates.csv")
    if exchange is None:
        self.exchange = {"GOOG": Stock("GOOG"), "AAPL":
            Stock("AAPL")}
    else:
        self.exchange = exchange
    rule_1 = PriceRule("GOOG", lambda stock: stock.price > 10)
    rule_2 = PriceRule("AAPL", lambda stock: stock.price > 5)
    self.exchange["GOOG"].updated.connect(
        lambda stock: self.print_action(stock, rule_1))
    self.exchange["AAPL"].updated.connect(
        lambda stock: self.print_action(stock, rule_2))
    if autorun:
        self.run()
```

And change the run method to call the reader:

```
def run(self):
    updates = self.reader.get_updates()
    self.do_updates(updates)
```

Notice how we are setting a default value so that other classes that use this class do not need to be changed. This allows us to override the `reader` parameter in tests as well as in new code, while the existing code will work fine without changes.

We can now write a test for this by passing in a mock object to the constructor:

```
def test_processor_gets_values_from_reader(self):
    mock_reader = mock.MagicMock()
    mock_reader.get_updates.return_value = \
        [('GOOG', datetime(2014, 2, 11, 14, 12, 22, 130000), 15)]
    processor = AlertProcessor(autorun=False, reader=mock_reader)
    processor.print_action = mock.Mock()
    processor.run()
    self.assertTrue(processor.print_action.called)
```

We can do the same by extracting the `print_action` method into an `Action` class and passing it in as a parameter.

Remember our original goals?

Right at the start of this chapter, we had said that we wanted to implement the following two features:

- We need to be able to get updates from a network server
- We need to be able to send an e-mail when an alert is matched

The original design didn't make it easy to add this functionality, and we would have needed to hack around the code—a dangerous and bug prone proposition.

Our newly refactored design now makes adding these features easy. All we need to do is to create new classes, say something like `NetworkReader`, which reads input from a server. We pass an instance of this object to the initializer via the reader parameter. `AlertProcessor` will then get updates from the server.

We can do the same with by implementing an `EmailAction` class and passing that object into this class.

# Long-term refactoring

We've managed to safely add the new features to our legacy code. But our work doesn't stop here. There are places where we added default parameters to the __init__ method so that we didn't break existing code that used this class. Over time, we would want to go to each of these places and change them to use the new interface. Once we have changed all the places, we can then remove the default parameters from the interface and the whole codebase would have migrated to the new interface.

The cool thing about this is that we don't have to do all the changes in one go. The codebase never stays broken for any length of time. We can make these changes over time, one by one, and the application is always working correctly at every point.

The other thing we need to do is to go back to our characterization tests and clean them up. Remember the first characterization test we wrote? It is as follows:

```python
import unittest
from unittest import mock


from ..legacy import AlertProcessor


class AlertProcessorTest(unittest.TestCase):
    @mock.patch("builtins.print")
    def test_processor_characterization_1(self, mock_print):
        AlertProcessor()
        mock_print.assert_has_calls([mock.call("AAPL", 8),
                                     mock.call("GOOG", 15),
                                     mock.call("AAPL", 10),
                                     mock.call("GOOG", 21)])
```

At the beginning of this chapter, we mentioned that this is not a great unit test, but it is good enough as a characterization test. Well, now is the time to revisit this test and make it better. Having refactored the design, we can now pass in a mock object for the reader. The test will no longer depend on the existence of the updates.csv file.

There were also a number of tests where we had patched out the print function. Once we refactor the design to take an Action class as an input, we would no longer need to patch this function as we can just pass in a mock action object to the initializer.

# Summary

In this chapter, you saw how to handle the hairy problem of working with the legacy code. We defined the legacy code as any code that does not contain tests. It is an unfortunate fact of life that we have to deal with such code. Fortunately there are a number of techniques available that allow us to safely work with such code. The interactive shell as well as the extremely powerful debugger are a huge help in understanding typical spaghetti code.

The dynamic nature of Python also makes it easy to break dependencies. We can use default value parameters to maintain compatibility with existing code while refactoring to a better design. Powerful patching features as well as the ability to dynamically alter existing instance variables and local methods allow us to write characterization tests that would normally have been much more difficult.

Now that you have seen many ways to write tests, let's look at ways to keep everything maintainable. We will do this in the next chapter.

# 6
# Maintaining Your Test Suite

If we do TDD regularly, we can easily end up with a large test suite containing thousands of tests. This is great—it gives us a lot of confidence to boldly go in and add new features without worrying about breaking old features. However, it is crucial that we make test maintenance easy, otherwise we will soon be in a mess just managing the tests.

Tests that are not written to be maintained will soon bring about a number of headaches. Tests that are strewn all over the filesystem will make it impossible to locate specific tests. Tests that are difficult to read will be hard to understand and fix when the tests need to be changed due to changes in functionality. Long, poorly written tests will pose the same challenges that poor production quality code does. And brittle tests will ensure that even small changes will break a large number of tests.

Remember that test code is still code. And just like any production code, we must do our best to keep it readable, maintainable, and easy to change. It is easy for us to fall into the trap of hacking out test cases and then forgetting about them. A year later, we find that maintaining the tests is a huge headache, and it is more difficult to add new features than it was before.

## Goals of test maintenance

As we have seen throughout this book, unit tests serve a number of different purposes:

- **Serve as a test suite**: This is the most obvious goal of unit tests. A comprehensive test suite reduces the number of bugs that can escape into production.

- **Serve as documentation**: When we are trying to understand what a class or method is trying to do, it is useful to take a look at the test suite. A well-written test suite will illustrate how the piece of code is supposed to behave.

- **Serve as a safety net**: This frees us from pressure when we refactor or clean up the code.
- **Illustrate the design**: Using mocks, we can depict the interactions between different classes or modules.

The goal of a well-written suite of unit tests is to enable these purposes as well as possible.

For example, if we want to understand what a method does, then we need to work out the following:

- Can we locate its unit test suite easily?
- Once located, is it easy to understand the tests and what they are testing for?
- Can we understand how this method interacts with other classes?
- Once we understand what the method does, then is it easy to refactor it? Does making small refactorings break all the tests?
- Is it easy to identify which tests have broken due to our refactoring and which failures are bugs in the refactoring?
- If we need to make changes in the test case due to the refactoring, then how difficult is it to understand the test and make the required change?

Any large, long-term project will involve answering all these questions.

Our goal in this chapter is to look at ways to make it easier to perform the preceding activities.

# Organizing tests

The first step in easing test maintenance is to have a systematic way of organizing tests. When we are implementing a new feature, we need to be able to quickly and easily locate the existing test code for a given method or class. There are three steps to making this easy. We have to decide:

- Where the files are stored on the filesystem
- What the files are called
- The names of the test classes

# Filesystem layout

The main consideration in deciding where to place our test code is the ease with which we can locate the tests for a specific class or module. Apart from this, there are two other considerations to keep in mind:

- How will this module be packaged and distributed?
- How will this code be put into production?

For the first consideration, we have to keep in mind that we will want to distribute unit tests along with the main code. For code that goes into production, we might not always want tests to be deployed, so we would be looking at a way to separate the code and tests.

Given all these considerations, there are two popular ways of laying out the test code.

In the first pattern, the test code is placed as a submodule of the main code like the following:

```
module
|
+- file
+- file
+- tests
   |
   + test_file
   + test_file
```

This allows us to package up both the module and the tests by just zipping up the module directory and putting it in an `egg` file. The whole package is self-contained and can be used directly. The module is accessed using an `import module` statement, and the tests are accessed by using `import module.tests`.

Running the tests also requires no configuration, as the tests can access the classes in the test code with relative imports such as `from ..file import class`.

This pattern is excellent for standalone modules that will be packaged in `egg` files and distributed.

The other pattern is to keep tests in a separate folder hierarchy altogether. The file layout will be something like the following:

```
root
|
+- module
|  |
|  +- file
|  +- file
|
+- tests
   |
   + test_file
   + test_file
```

The preceding pattern is suitable for situations where there is a need to separate out the tests from the code. This could be because we are making a product and don't want to send tests to our customers, or it could be because we don't want to deploy tests to the production servers. This pattern is suitable because it is easy to zip up the module alone into an egg file and deploy.

The downside of the pattern is that if the project involves many modules, then it can be troublesome to separate out tests for the different modules. One pattern is to use different roots for each directory, as shown in the following:

```
root
|
+- src
|  |
|  +- module1
|  |  |
|  |  +- file
|  |  +- file
|
+- tests
   |
   +- module1
      |
      + test_file
      + test_file
```

The preceding pattern is commonly seen in languages such as Java, but it is overall quite cumbersome and verbose. However, it could be a solution for specific needs like the ones mentioned previously.

Two patterns we definitely *don't* want to do are as follows:

- Place the tests in the same file as the code
- Place the test files in the same directory as the code

Placing tests in the same file as code is okay for single file scripts, but it is messy for anything bigger than that. The problem is that if the file is long, then it becomes very difficult to navigate the file. And since tests often need to import other classes, it pollutes the namespace. It also increases the chances for circular imports. Finally, it makes it difficult to execute all the tests at once because the test runners look for patterns in the filename.

As for placing files in the same directory, it once again messes up the module, making it difficult to find files in the directory. It doesn't have any specific advantages apart from not having to create a separate tests directory. Avoid this pattern and create a submodule instead.

# Naming conventions

The next step is to decide on a naming convention for test files, test classes, and test methods.

For test files, it is best to go with the `test_` prefix for the file. For example, a file called `file1.py` will have its tests in `test_file1.py`. This makes it easy for us to locate the corresponding test code when we are looking at some production code. Having the `test_` prefix is preferable because this is the default pattern that is searched by most test runners. If we use some other prefix, or use a suffix like `file1_test.py`, then most probably we will have to pass additional configuration into the test runner to find and execute the tests. This extra configuration is easily avoidable by just sticking to the default convention that is expected from most of the commonly used tools.

For example, we can run the tests with the following command:

```
python3 -m unittest discover
```

But if we were to name our tests with a suffix of `_test`, then we have to use the following command:

```
python3 -m unittest discover -p *_test.py
```

It works, but it is just extra configuration that can be avoided. We should use this only if we have a legacy naming convention that needs to be preserved.

What about test classes and test methods? The `unittest` module looks at all classes that inherit from `unittest.TestCase`. So, the class name does not matter. However, other test runners such as `nose2` also pick up test classes based on the name of the class. The default pattern is to search for classes that end with `Test`. It therefore makes sense to name all the test classes to end with `Test`. It is also descriptive, so there really is no good reason to do anything else.

Similarly, test methods should start with `test`. This is the default pattern that test runners search for, and once again it makes sense to just stick to this convention. Methods that do not start with `test` can be used as helper methods.

# Test suite grouping

Finally, we come to the question of what a class should contain—should one test class contain tests for a target class, or should we store all the tests for a method in a test class? Here, it is more a question of personal preference. Neither is objectively better or worse, it just depends on which is more readable. My personal preference is to use both patterns within a single codebase, depending on how many tests there are and which pattern makes it easier to find the tests that I am looking for. In general, if there are a lot of tests for a single method, then I would refactor them into a separate test class.

# Making tests readable

In the previous section, we looked at the rather mundane issue of file layout and naming conventions. We are now going to take a look at the ways we can improve the test cases themselves.

Our first goal is to make it easier to understand the tests themselves. There is nothing worse than locating a test case and then having a hard time figuring out what the test is trying to do.

I'm sure I will not be the first to confess that there have been multiple occasions where I have returned to a test that I myself wrote a year back, and struggled to understand what I was trying to do.

This is an area that is often ignored because when we write the test, it seems perfectly obvious what the test does. We will need to put ourselves in the shoes of someone who is looking at the test for the first time or after a couple of years and trying to understand the test without having the contextual knowledge that we had while writing the test. This is a recurring problem when working on large codebases.

# Using docstrings

The first line of defense for an unreadable test is to use a docstring. **Docstrings** are a great feature of Python because they are available at runtime. Test runners typically pick up a docstring and display it during test errors and failures, making it easy to see what is failing from the test report itself.

Some people will say that a well-written test has no need for additional explanation. In fact, we said something similar in *Chapter 3, Code Smells and Refactoring* when we discussed the value of comments. To repeat what we said there: there is no value in comments that explain what is going on, but there is value in comments that explain why we have implemented the code as we have. The same principle applies to docstrings as well.

For example, take a look at the following code:

```python
def get_closing_price_list(self, on_date, num_days):
    closing_price_list = []
    for i in range(num_days):
        chk = on_date.date() - timedelta(i)
        for price_event in reversed(self.series):
            if price_event.timestamp.date() > chk:
                pass
            if price_event.timestamp.date() == chk:
                closing_price_list.insert(0, price_event)
                break
            if price_event.timestamp.date() < chk:
                closing_price_list.insert(0, price_event)
                break
    return closing_price_list
```

This is the `get_closing_price_list` method from the `TimeSeries` class that we refactored in *Chapter 3, Code Smells and Refactoring*. The following is a test for that method:

```python
class TimeSeriesTest(unittest.TestCase):
    def test_closing_price_list_before_series_start_date(self):
        series = TimeSeries()
        series.update(datetime(2014, 3, 10), 5)
        on_date = datetime(2014, 3, 9)
        self.assertEqual([],
            series.get_closing_price_list(on_date, 1))
```

This test checks that an empty list is returned when the date passed is before the start of the timeseries. This is quite clear from the test. But why does it return an empty list instead of, say, throwing an exception? A docstring provides a good place to explain this design decision, as shown in the following:

```python
def test_closing_price_list_before_series_start_date(self):
    """
    Empty list is returned if on_date is before the start of the
    series
    The moving average calculation might be done before any data
    has been added to the stock. We return an empty list so that
    the calculation can still proceed as usual.
    """
    series = TimeSeries()
    series.update(datetime(2014, 3, 10), 5)
    on_date = datetime(2014, 3, 9)
    self.assertEqual([],
        series.get_closing_price_list(on_date, 1))
```

# Using fixtures

Having looked at docstrings, we can now turn our attention to the tests themselves.

If we look at the general structure of unit tests, they generally follow the Arrange-Act-Assert structure. Of these, the Act section is usually only a couple of lines and the Assert section is also a few lines at most. By far the biggest part of the test is in the Arrange section. For more complex tests, where a specific scenario might take many lines to set up, the Arrange section could easily be 75 percent to 80 percent of the whole test.

One way of avoiding repetitive code is to move it all into the appropriate `setUp` and `tearDown` methods. As we saw in *Chapter 2, Red-Green-Refactor – The TDD Cycle*, `unittest` provides three levels of setup and teardown methods:

- `setUp` and `tearDown` that are run before and after each test
- `setUpClass` and `tearDownClass` that are run before and after each test class
- `setUpModule` and `tearDownModule` that are run before and after each test file

This method of setting up the data for a test is called a **fixture**. Using fixtures is a good idea to reduce common code duplication between tests. However, there are some downsides to be aware of:

- Sometimes, there is a lot of setup to be done, but each of the tests only use a small part of the overall fixture. In this case, it can be confusing for a new developer to figure out which part of the fixture is used by each test.

- We have to be careful when using class- and module-level fixtures. Because the fixture is shared between multiple tests, we have to be careful that we don't change the state of the fixture. If we do, then there is the possibility that the result of one test could alter the fixture state for the next. This could lead to very strange bugs when tests are executed in a different order.

One thing to be aware of is that if the `setUp` method throws an exception, then the `tearDown` method is not called. Take the following example:

```
class SomeTest(unittest.TestCase):
    def setUp(self):
        connect_to_database()
        connect_to_server()


    def tearDown(self):
        disconnect_from_database()
        disconnect_from_server()
```

If an exception is raised in the `connect_to_server` call, then the `tearDown` method will not be called. This will leave the connection to the database hanging open. When `setUp` is called for the next test, the first line might fail (because the connection is already open), causing all the other tests to fail.

To avoid this situation, the `unittest` module provides the `addCleanup` method. This method takes a callback function, which is called no matter whether the setup passed or failed, as shown in the following:

```
class SomeTest2(unittest.TestCase):
    def setUp(self):
        connect_to_database()
        self.addCleanup(self.disconnect_database)
        connect_to_server()
        self.addCleanup(self.disconnect_server)


    def disconnect_database(self):
```

```
        disconnect_from_database()


    def disconnect_server(self):
        disconnect_from_server()
```

With this structure, how execution will flow is given as follows:

- If the database call failed, then no cleanup will be performed
- If the database call succeeded but the server call failed, then `disconnect_database` will be called during cleanup
- If both calls succeeded, then both `disconnect_database` and `disconnect_server` will be called during cleanup

When would we use `addCleanup` versus `tearDown`? In general, when accessing resources that must be closed, `addCleanup` is the way to go. `tearDown` is a good place to put other types of cleanup, or in cases where `setUp` cannot throw an exception.

# Fixtures and patching

There is one complication in using patched mocks along with fixtures. Take a look at the following code:

```
@mock.patch.object(smtplib, "SMTP")
class EmailActionTest(unittest.TestCase):
    def setUp(self):
        self.action =
            EmailAction(to="siddharta@silverstripesoftware.com")


    def test_connection_closed_after_sending_mail(self,
        mock_smtp_class):
        mock_smtp = mock_smtp_class.return_value
        self.action.execute("MSFT has crossed $10 price level")
        mock_smtp.send_message.assert_called_with(mock.ANY)
        self.assertTrue(mock_smtp.quit.called)
        mock_smtp.assert_has_calls([
            mock.call.send_message(mock.ANY),
            mock.call.quit()])
```

This is one of the tests for the `EmailAction` class that we looked at earlier. The `patch` decorator is used at a class level to patch the `smtplib.SMTP` class and pass the mock as a parameter to all the test cases. Because of the way the patch decorator works, it only passes the mock to the test case methods, which means that we cannot access it in our `setUp` method.

If we look at this test, it uses the `mock_smtp` object, which is derived from `mock_smtp_class`. The line that gets the `mock_smtp` object can be moved into the `setUp` method, if only we could access `mock_smtp_class` over there. Is there a way by which we can apply the patch in the `setUp` method so that we can do some common setup with the mock?

Fortunately, the `unittest` module gives us the tools to do just this. Instead of using the decorator syntax for patching, we will use the regular object syntax like the following:

```
def setUp(self):
    patcher = mock.patch("smtplib.SMTP")
    self.addCleanup(patcher.stop)
    self.mock_smtp_class = patcher.start()
    self.mock_smtp = self.mock_smtp_class.return_value
    self.action =
        EmailAction(to="siddharta@silverstripesoftware.com")
```

What we are doing here is passing the object to be patched—in this case `smtplib.SMTP`—to the `patch` function. This returns a patcher object with two methods: `start` and `stop`. When we call the `start` method, the patch is applied, and when we call the `stop` method, the patch is removed.

We set the `patcher.stop` method to be executed during the test cleanup phase by passing it to the `addCleanup` function. We then start the patch. The `start` method returns the mock object, which we use for the rest of the setup.

With this setup, we can use `self.mock_smtp` directly in our tests, without having to get it from `mock_smtp_class` in every test. The test would now look like the following:

```
def test_connection_closed_after_sending_mail(self):
    self.action.execute("MSFT has crossed $10 price level")
    self.mock_smtp.send_message.assert_called_with(mock.ANY)
    self.assertTrue(self.mock_smtp.quit.called)
    self.mock_smtp.assert_has_calls([
        mock.call.send_message(mock.ANY),
        mock.call.quit()])
```

Compare this test with the one earlier in this section. Since we are not using the decorator patch syntax, we no longer need the extra parameter. We also don't need to derive mock_smtp from mock_smtp_class in every test. Instead, all that work is done in setUp. The test can then access self.mock_smtp and use it directly.

# Using a custom test case class hierarchy

One more way of reducing code duplication is to create our own test class hierarchy. For example, if a helper method is used often in many test classes, then we can pull it up to a higher class and inherit test classes from that instead. The following is an example to make the concept clearer:

```
class MyTestCase(unittest.TestCase):
    def create_start_object(self, value):
        do_something(value)


class SomeTest(MyTestCase):
    def test_1(self):
        create_start_object("value 1")


class SomeTest2(MyTestCase):
    def test_2(self):
        create_start_object("value 2")


    def test_3(self):
        create_start_object("value 3")
```

In this example, we create a class called MyTestCase that inherits from unittest. TestCase, and we put in some helper methods in this class. The actual test classes inherit from MyTestCase and can access the helper methods that are in the parent class.

Using this technique, we can take common groups of helper methods and put them into reusable parent classes. The hierarchy need not be only one level deep; sometimes, we might create further subclasses for specific areas of the application that we are testing.

# Writing tests closer to the domain

The other way to make tests easier to read is to write tests in terms of the domain language instead of just the generic functions provided by `unittest`. In this section, we look at some ways to do this.

# Writing helper methods

The first technique is to write helper methods. We employed this technique earlier in this book. The following are some tests that don't use a helper method:

```
def test_increasing_trend_is_false_if_price_decreases(self):
    timestamps = [datetime(2014, 2, 11), datetime(2014, 2, 12),
                    datetime(2014, 2, 13)]
    prices = [8, 12, 10]
    for timestamp, price in zip(timestamps, prices):
        self.goog.update(timestamp, price)
    self.assertFalse(self.goog.is_increasing_trend())


def test_increasing_trend_is_false_if_price_equal(self):
    timestamps = [datetime(2014, 2, 11), datetime(2014, 2, 12),
                    datetime(2014, 2, 13)]
    prices = [8, 10, 10]
    for timestamp, price in zip(timestamps, prices):
        self.goog.update(timestamp, price)
    self.assertFalse(self.goog.is_increasing_trend())
```

While the tests are short, it isn't really clear what is happening in the tests. Let's move some of that code into a helper method, as shown in the following:

```
def given_a_series_of_prices(self, prices):
    timestamps = [datetime(2014, 2, 10), datetime(2014, 2, 11),
                    datetime(2014, 2, 12), datetime(2014, 2, 13)]
    for timestamp, price in zip(timestamps, prices):
    self.goog.update(timestamp, price)
```

The following are the same two tests using the new helper method:

```
def test_increasing_trend_is_false_if_price_decreases(self):
    self.given_a_series_of_prices([8, 12, 10])
    self.assertFalse(self.goog.is_increasing_trend())


def test_increasing_trend_is_false_if_price_equal(self):
    self.given_a_series_of_prices([8, 10, 10])
    self.assertFalse(self.goog.is_increasing_trend())
```

As we can see, the tests are a lot clearer now. This is because the helper method clearly expresses the intent of the calculation, making it easy for a new developer to correlate the steps in the test case with their mental model of the requirements.

# Writing better asserts

An easy way to enhance test readability is to write our own assert methods that are higher level than the generic asserts provided by unittest. For example, suppose we wanted to write a test to verify the price history of a stock. The following is how such a test might look:

```
class TimeSeriesEqualityTest(unittest.TestCase):
    def test_timeseries_price_history(self):
        series = TimeSeries()
        series.update(datetime(2014, 3, 10), 5)
        series.update(datetime(2014, 3, 11), 15)
        self.assertEqual(5, series[0].value)
        self.assertEqual(15, series[1].value)
```

Now, another way to write the test is as follows:

```
class TimeSeriesTestCase(unittest.TestCase):
    def assert_has_price_history(self, price_list, series):
        for index, expected_price in enumerate(price_list):
            actual_price = series[index].value
            if actual_price != expected_price:
                raise self.failureException("[%d]: %d !=
                    %d".format(index, expected_price, actual_price))


class TimeSeriesEqualityTest(TimeSeriesTestCase):
    def test_timeseries_price_history(self):
```

```
    series = TimeSeries()
    series.update(datetime(2014, 3, 10), 5)
    series.update(datetime(2014, 3, 11), 15)
    self.assert_has_price_history([5, 15], series)
```

In the preceding example, we have created our own base test class and with a custom assert method. The test case inherits from this base test class and uses the assert in the test.

The implementation of the `assert_has_price_history` method gives an idea of how simple it is to write our own assert methods. All we have to do is to implement our assertion logic, and raise `self.failureException` whenever the assert should signal a test failure. `self.failureException` is an attribute of `unittest.TestCase`, and it is usually set to the `AssertionError` exception. We could raise `AssertionError` ourselves, but the `unittest` module allows us to configure using a different exception, so it is best to raise `self.failureException`, which is always set to the correct value to be used.

When the same sequence of asserts is made again and again in multiple tests, we should see whether there is an opportunity to replace the calls to the built-in asserts with a higher level assert that more clearly expresses the intent that we want to convey.

# Using custom equality checkers

A cool feature of the `assertEqual` method is the way it gives custom failure messages depending on the type of object being compared. If we try to assert two integers, the following is what we get:

```
>>> import unittest
>>> testcase = unittest.TestCase()
>>> testcase.assertEqual(1, 2)
Traceback (most recent call last):

    ...

AssertionError: 1 != 2
```

On the other hand, asserting lists gives us another message showing the difference in the expected and actual lists, as shown in the following:

```
>>> import unittest
>>> testcase = unittest.TestCase()
>>> testcase.assertEqual([1, 2], [1, 3])
Traceback (most recent call last):
```

```
. . .
AssertionError: Lists differ: [1, 2] != [1, 3]

First differing element 1:
2
3

- [1, 2]
?      ^

+ [1, 3]
?      ^
```

Under the hood, `assertEqual` delegates to a different function depending on the type of object being compared. This is how we get specific and relevant equality checks for most common built-in data structures such as strings, sequences, lists, tuples, sets, and dicts.

Fortunately, this flexible system is open to use by developers, which means we can add our own equality checkers for our application objects. The following is a default scenario where we try to compare two `Stock` objects:

```
>>> import unittest
>>> from stock_alerter.stock import Stock
>>> test_case = unittest.TestCase()
>>> stock_1 = Stock("GOOG")
>>> stock_2 = Stock("GOOG")
>>> test_case.assertEqual(stock_1, stock_2)
Traceback (most recent call last):
    . . .
AssertionError: <stock_alerter.stock.Stock object at 0x000000000336EDD8>
!= <stock_alerter.stock.Stock object at 0x00000000033E9588>
```

The assertion fails because although both objects contain the same data, they are still different objects in memory. Now let's try to register our own equality function for the `Stock` class that just compares the symbol to identify equality between `Stock` objects. All we have to do is to register our checker using the `addTypeEqualityFunc` method like the following:

```
>>> test_case.addTypeEqualityFunc(Stock, lambda stock_1, stock_2, msg:
stock_1.symbol == stock_2.symbol)
```

```
>>> test_case.assertEqual(stock_1, stock_2)
>>> print(test_case.assertEqual(stock_1, stock_2))
None
>>>
```

The equality checker takes three parameters: the first object, the second object, and the optional message that the user passed to assertEqual. Once we register the function like this, we can call assertEqual passing in two Stock objects and assertEqual will delegate the comparison to the function that we registered.

Using equality functions this way is a nice way to assert application domain objects in the unit test code. This method has two limitations though:

- We have to use the same comparison function for a given type. There is no way to use one comparison function in some tests and another comparison function in other tests.
- Both parameters to assertEqual have to be objects of that type. There is no way we can pass in two objects of differing types.

Both these limitations can be overcome using matchers, which is what we will now turn our attention to.

# Using matchers

A third way to make asserts more readable is to create custom matcher objects to make comparisons more readable during assertions. We saw a glimpse of using matchers while writing tests for the EmailAction class earlier. The following is a look at that matcher again:

```python
class MessageMatcher:
    def __init__(self, expected):
        self.expected = expected

    def __eq__(self, other):
        return self.expected["Subject"] == other["Subject"] and \
            self.expected["From"] == other["From"] and \
            self.expected["To"] == other["To"] and \
            self.expected["Message"] == other._payload
```

A matcher can be any class that implements the __eq__ method. The method will take the actual object as a parameter and the method can implement any comparison logic required. Using this method, we can directly compare domain objects in the assertion without cluttering it with a number of separate asserts.

The matcher does not need to compare complete domain objects. We can compare only the attributes that we are interested in. In fact, we can create different matchers to match against specific subsets of objects. For example, we might create an `AlertMessageMatcher` like the following:

```
class AlertMessageMatcher:
    def __init__(self, expected):
        self.expected = expected

    def __eq__(self, other):
        return self.expected["Subject"] == "New Stock Alert" and \
            self.expected["From"] == other["From"] and \
            self.expected["To"] == other["To"] and \
            self.expected["Message"] == other._payload
```

This matcher will only match alert messages that have the given subject, while taking the other parameters from the expected object.

# Summary

In this chapter, you looked a little more in detail at the important but often overlooked topic of keeping tests maintainable. You looked at the importance of having a consistent test file layout scheme and the pros and cons of various alternatives. You looked at naming tests and grouping tests, before moving to the topic of making tests easier to understand. Some of the strategies that we discussed were using docstrings, creating custom test class hierarchies, and utilizing fixtures. Finally, you looked at making code more readable by using helper functions, custom asserts, equality functions, and writing custom matchers.

In the next chapter, you will look at incorporating tests in your documentation using the doctest module.

# Executable Documentation
## with doctest

Throughout this book, we have emphasized the need for code to be self-documenting as far as possible. We have mentioned how the cool docstring feature of Python helps us in this objective. There is one problem with documentation in general—it can easily go out of sync with the code. Many times we have seen changes to the code, but the corresponding change is not made to the documentation, leaving a new developer confused about how the code actually works. Enter the doctest module to our rescue.

The doctest module allows us to specify examples inside our docstrings. The module then extracts the examples, runs them, and verifies that they still work.

## Our first doctest

The following is the current version of the price method in the Stock class:

```
def price(self):
    try:
        return self.history[-1].value
    except IndexError:
        return None
```

Now, in the docstring, we add an example of how this method might be used. The examples are basically a copy-paste of a Python interactive shell. Hence, the lines containing input to be executed are prefixed with >>> prompt, and the lines without the prompt indicate output, as shown in the following:

```
def price(self):
    """Returns the current price of the Stock


    >>> from datetime import datetime
    >>> stock = Stock("GOOG")
    >>> stock.update(datetime(2011, 10, 3), 10)
    >>> stock.price
    10
    """

    try:
        return self.history[-1].value
    except IndexError:
        return None
```

Now that we have the docstring, we need a way to execute it. Add the following lines to the bottom of the file:

```
if __name__ == "__main__":
    import doctest
    doctest.testmod()
```

# Running the doctest

Now we can run the tests by executing the file as a module. We need to execute the file as a module so that the relative imports work. If this was a standalone script, or we used absolute imports instead of relative imports, then we could have just directly executed the file. Since the code above is in the stock.py file, we have to execute the stock_alerter.stock module. The following is the command to execute it:

- Windows: python.exe -m stock_alerter.stock
- Linux/Mac: python3 -m stock_alerter.stock

When we run the above command, we'll get the output as nothing. Yes, nothing. If there is no output, then it means that all the doctests passed. We can pass the -v command line parameter (for verbose output) to see that the test indeed passed as follows:

- Windows: `python.exe -m stock_alerter.stock -v`
- Linux/Mac: `python3 -m stock_alerter.stock -v`

When we do this, we get the following output:

```
Trying:
    from datetime import datetime
Expecting nothing
ok
Trying:
    stock = Stock("GOOG")
Expecting nothing
ok
Trying:
    stock.update(datetime(2011, 10, 3), 10)
Expecting nothing
ok
Trying:
    stock.price
Expecting:
    10
ok
8 items had no tests:
    __main__
    __main__.Stock
    __main__.Stock.__init__
    __main__.Stock._is_crossover_below_to_above
    __main__.Stock.get_crossover_signal
    __main__.Stock.is_increasing_trend
    __main__.Stock.update
    __main__.StockSignal
1 items passed all tests:
    4 tests in __main__.Stock.price
```

```
4 tests in 9 items.
4 passed and 0 failed.
Test passed.
```

Let us look at that output in a little more detail.

If we look at the first line of our example, it contains the following:

```
>>> from datetime import datetime
```

doctest picks up this line and evaluates the output:

```
Trying:
    from datetime import datetime
Expecting nothing
ok
```

The next line of the example is another input line starting with the >>> prompt, so doctest figures that executing the first line should not have any output, hence the statement *Expecting nothing*.

When this first line of the test is executed, indeed nothing is printed, so doctest gives the output *ok*, meaning that the line executed as expected. doctest then goes on to the next line and follows the same procedure until the following line is encountered:

```
>>> stock.price
10
```

Our test says that, when this line is executed, the output of 10 should be printed. That is exactly what doctest checks for as well, as shown in the following:

```
Trying:
    stock.price
Expecting:
    10
ok
```

> Note that we don't explicitly call print(stock.price). We just put stock.price and expect the output of 10. This is exactly the behavior we see in the Python interactive shell; doctest uses the same behavior.

After this line, our example ends and `doctest` continues on to the next method, as shown in the following:

```
8 items had no tests:
    __main__
    __main__.Stock
    __main__.Stock.__init__
    __main__.Stock._is_crossover_below_to_above
    __main__.Stock.get_crossover_signal
    __main__.Stock.is_increasing_trend
    __main__.Stock.update
    __main__.StockSignal
1 items passed all tests:
    4 tests in __main__.Stock.price
4 tests in 9 items.
4 passed and 0 failed.
Test passed.
```

It tells us that the remaining methods didn't have tests, and that all the tests passed. Note that `doctest` counts each line of the example as a separate test, hence the reason why it identified four tests. Since Python supports module-level and class-level docstrings, we could have put some examples in those as well, perhaps examples on how to use the module or the class as a whole. This is why `doctest` also tells us that `__main__` and `__main__.Stock` do not have any tests.

The beauty of doctests is that it allows us to mix documentation between the examples. This allows us to expand the docstring for the `price` method like the following:

```
def price(self):
    """Returns the current price of the Stock

    >>> from datetime import datetime
    >>> stock = Stock("GOOG")
    >>> stock.update(datetime(2011, 10, 3), 10)
    >>> stock.price
```

```
10
```

The method will return the latest price by timestamp, so even
if updates are out of order, it will return the latest one

```
>>> stock = Stock("GOOG")
>>> stock.update(datetime(2011, 10, 3), 10)
```

Now, let us do an update with a date that is earlier than the
previous one

```
>>> stock.update(datetime(2011, 10, 2), 5)
```

And the method still returns the latest price

```
>>> stock.price
10
```

If there are no updates, then the method returns None

```
>>> stock = Stock("GOOG")
>>> print(stock.price)
None
"""
try:
    return self.history[-1].value
except IndexError:
    return None
```

Run the above and it should pass with the following new output:

```
Trying:
    stock = Stock("GOOG")
Expecting nothing
ok
Trying:
    stock.update(datetime(2011, 10, 3), 10)
```

```
Expecting nothing
ok
Trying:
    stock.update(datetime(2011, 10, 2), 5)
Expecting nothing
ok
Trying:
    stock.price
Expecting:
    10
ok
Trying:
    stock = Stock("GOOG")
Expecting nothing
ok
Trying:
    print(stock.price)
Expecting:
    None
ok
```

As we can see, doctest goes through the documentation and identifies the exact lines that need to be executed. This allows us to put explanations and documentation in between the code snippets. The result? Well-explained documentation plus testable code. A great combination!

Let us take one quick look at the last example:

```
>>> stock = Stock("GOOG")
>>> print(stock.price)
None
```

If you notice, we explicitly print the output. The reason is that the Python interactive shell usually does not give any output when the value is None. Since doctest mimics the behavior of the interactive shell, we could have just had an empty line and the test would have passed, but it is not really clear what is happening. So, we call print to make it explicit that we are expecting None as the output.

# Test failures

Let us now see what a test failure looks like. The following is a doctest for the
is_increasing_trend method:

```
def is_increasing trend(self):
    """Returns True if the past three values have been strictly
    increasing

    Returns False if there have been less than three updates
    so far

    >>> stock = Stock("GOOG")
    >>> stock.is_increasing_trend()
    False
    """

    return self.history[-3].value < \
        self.history[-2].value < self.history[-1].value
```

The following is what we get when we run the test:

```
Failed example:
    stock.is_increasing_trend()
Exception raised:
    Traceback (most recent call last):
      File "C:\Python34\lib\doctest.py", line 1324, in __run
        compileflags, 1), test.globs)
      File "<doctest __main__.Stock.is_increasing_trend[1]>", line 1, in
<module>
        stock.is_increasing_trend()
      File "c:\Projects\tdd_with_python\src\stock_alerter\stock.py", line
91, in is_increasing_trend
        return self.history[-3].value < \
      File "c:\Projects\tdd with_python\src\stock_alerter\timeseries.py",
line 13, in __getitem__
        return self.series[index]
    IndexError: list index out of range
```

```
***********************************************************************
1 items had failures:
   1 of   2 in __main__.Stock.is_increasing_trend
***Test Failed*** 1 failures.
```

doctest tells us which line caused the failure. It also tells us which command was executed, and what happened. We can see that an unexpected exception has failed the test.

We can now fix the code as follows:

```
def is_increasing_trend(self):
    """Returns True if the past three values have been strictly
    increasing

    Returns False if there have been less than three updates
    so far

    >>> stock = Stock("GOOG")
    >>> stock.is_increasing_trend()
    False
    """

    try:
        return self.history[-3].value < \
            self.history[-2].value < self.history[-1].value
    except IndexError:
        return True
```

The exception is now gone, but we have a bug in the fix because it has been replaced with a failure, as shown in the following:

```
Failed example:
    stock.is_increasing_trend()
Expected:
    False
Got:
    True
```

Let's fix it:

```
def is_increasing_trend(self):
    """Returns True if the past three values have been strictly
    increasing

    Returns False if there have been less than three updates so
    far

    >>> stock = Stock("GOOG")
    >>> stock.is_increasing_trend()
    False
    """

    try:
        return self.history[-3].value < \
            self.history[-2].value < self.history[-1].value
    except IndexError:
        return False
```

With this fix, all the tests are passing again.

# Testing for exceptions

The update method should also raise a ValueError when the price is less than zero.
The following is how we verify this in the doctest:

```
def update(self, timestamp, price):
    """Updates the stock with the price at the given timestamp

    >>> from datetime import datetime
    >>> stock = Stock("GOOG")
    >>> stock.update(datetime(2014, 10, 2), 10)
    >>> stock.price
    10

    The method raises a ValueError exception if the price is
    negative

    >>> stock.update(datetime(2014, 10, 2), -1)
```

```
    Traceback (most recent call last):

      ...

    ValueError: price should not be negative
    """

    if price < 0:
        raise ValueError("price should not be negative")
    self.history.update(timestamp, price)
    self.updated.fire(self)
```

The next section shows the expectation that doctest looks at:

```
Traceback (most recent call last):

  ...

ValueError: price should not be negative
```

The expected output starts with the regular traceback output. This line tells doctest that an exception is expected. After that comes the actual traceback. Since the output often contains file paths that might change, it is very hard to match it exactly. Fortunately, we don't need to. doctest allows us to put three indented dots to signify the middle part of the traceback. Finally, the last line shows the expected exception and the exception message. This is the line that is matched to see whether the test passed or failed.

# Package-level doctests

As we have seen so far, doctests can be written for methods, classes, and modules. However, they can also be written for whole packages. Typically, these would be put in the __init__.py file of the package and would show how the package as a whole should work, including multiple interacting classes. Here is one such set of doctests from our __init__.py file:

```
r"""
The stock_alerter module allows you to set up rules and get alerted
when those rules are met.


>>> from datetime import datetime


First, we need to setup an exchange that contains all the stocks that
are going to be processed. A simple dictionary will do.


>>> from stock_alerter.stock import Stock
```

```
>>> exchange = {"GOOG": Stock("GOOG"), "AAPL": Stock("AAPL")}
```

Next, we configure the reader. The reader is the source from where the stock updates are coming. The module provides two readers out of the box: A FileReader for reading updates from a comma separated file, and a ListReader to get updates from a list. You can create other readers, such as an HTTPReader, to get updates from a remote server.

Here we create a simple ListReader by passing in a list of 3-tuples containing the stock symbol, timestamp and price.

```
>>> from stock_alerter.reader import ListReader
>>> reader = ListReader([("GOOG", datetime(2014, 2, 8), 5)])
```

Next, we set up an Alert. We give it a rule, and an action to be taken when the rule is fired.

```
>>> from stock_alerter.alert import Alert
>>> from stock_alerter.rule import PriceRule
>>> from stock_alerter.action import PrintAction
>>> alert = Alert("GOOG > $3", PriceRule("GOOG",
lambda s: s.price > 3),\
...                PrintAction())
```

Connect the alert to the exchange

```
>>> alert.connect(exchange)
```

Now that everything is setup, we can start processing the updates

```
>>> from stock_alerter.processor import Processor
>>> processor = Processor(reader, exchange)
>>> processor.process()
GOOG > $3
"""


if __name__ == "__main__":
    import doctest
    doctest.testmod()
```

We can run it like the following:

- **Windows**: `python.exe -m stock_alerter.__init__`
- **Linux/Mac**: `python3 -m stock_alerter.__init__`

When we do this, the tests pass.

There are a few things to note about this test:

We are using absolute imports instead of relative imports in the doctest. For example, we say `from stock_alerter.stock import Stock` instead of `from .stock import Stock`. This allows us to easily run doctests from the command line. An alternate way to run this doctest is as follows:

- **Windows**: `python.exe -m doctest stock_alerter\__init__.py`
- **Linux/Mac**: `python3 -m doctest stock_alerter\__init__.py`

This syntax only works if the file is using absolute imports. Otherwise, we'll get the error `SystemError: Parent module '' not loaded, cannot perform relative import`.

Generally, when doing package level doctests, using absolute imports is recommended.

Apart from that, some of the examples also continue across multiple lines. The following is one such example:

```
>>> alert = Alert("GOOG > $3", PriceRule("GOOG", lambda s: s.price > 3),\
...                 PrintAction())
```

The way to support multiple lines is just the same as in the interactive shell. End the line with a backslash \ and start the next line with three dots . . . . This is interpreted by `doctest` as a line continuation and it will combine both lines into a single input.

 **An important gotcha**: Notice that the docstring starts with the r prefix, like this `r"""`. This indicates a raw string. As mentioned above, we have used the backslash in a few places to indicate continuation of input. When Python finds a backslash in a string, it interprets it as an escape character instead of a literal backslash. The solution is to either escape the backslash by putting a double backslash \ \ or to use a raw string in which no backslash interpretation is done. Rather than putting double backslashes everywhere, it is preferable to use a raw string by marking the start of the docstring with the r prefix.

# Maintaining doctests

Doctests can be quite verbose, often containing a lot of explanation mixed in with the examples. These doctests can easily run into multiple pages. Sometimes, there could be many lines of doctests followed by just a few lines of code. We can see this happening in our `update` method. This can make navigating the code more difficult.

We can solve this problem by putting the doctests into a separate file. Suppose, we put the contents of the docstring into a file called `readme.txt`. We then change our `__init__.py` file like the following:

```
if __name__ == "__main__":
    import doctest
    doctest.testfile("readme.txt")
```

This will now load the contents of `readme.txt` and run it as doctests.

When writing tests in an external file, there is no need to put quotes around the contents as we would in a Python file. The entire file content is considered as doctests. Similarly, we also do not need to escape backslashes.

This feature makes it practical to just put all doctests into separate files. These files should double up as user documentation and contain the doctests in them. This way, we avoid cluttering up the actual code with pages and pages of doctrings.

# Running a suite of doctests

One of the missing features of the `doctest` module is an effective autodiscovery mechanism. Unlike `unittest` that searches all files for tests and runs them, with doctest we have to execute each file explicitly on the command line. This is a big pain for large projects.

There are some ways to accomplish this, though. The most straightforward is to wrap the doctest into a `unittest.TestCase` class, like the following:

```
import doctest
import unittest
from stock_alerter import stock


class PackageDocTest(unittest.TestCase):
```

```
    def test_stock_module(self):
        doctest.testmod(stock)


    def test_doc(self):
        doctest.testfile(r"..\readme.txt")
```

These doctests can then be run along with the rest of the unit tests as usual.

This works, but the problem is that the test doesn't fail if there is a failure in the doctest. The error is printed out, but it doesn't record a failure. This is okay if the tests are run manually, but causes a problem when the tests are run in an automated fashion, for example, as a part of a build or deploy process.

`doctest` has another feature by which it can be wrapped inside a `unittest`:

```
import doctest
from stock_alerter import stock


def load_tests(loader, tests, pattern):
    tests.addTests(doctest.DocTestSuite(stock))
    tests.addTests(doctest.DocFileSuite("../readme.txt"))
    return tests
```

We haven't looked at `load_tests` before, so let us take a quick look now. `load_tests` is used by the `unittest` module to load the unit tests suites from the current module. When this function is not present, `unittest` uses its default method of loading tests by looking for classes that inherit from `unittest.TestCase`. However, when this function is present, it is called and it can return a different suite of tests from the default. The returned suite is then run.

Since doctests aren't part of `unittest.TestCase`, they are not run by default when we execute the unit tests. What we do instead is implement the `load_tests` function and add the doctests to the test suite in that function. We use the `doctest.DocTestSuite` and `doctest.DocFileSuite` methods to create `unittest`-compatible test suites from the doctests. We then append these test suites to the overall tests to be executed in the `load_tests` function.

`doctest.DocTestSuite` takes the module containing the tests as a parameter.

 Note that we have to pass in the actual module object, and not just a string.

`doctest.DocFileSuite` takes a filename containing the doctests. The filename is relative to the current test module's directory. So, for example, if our directory structure is like the following:

```
src
|
+- stock_alerter
   |
   +- readme.txt
   +- tests
      |
      +- test_doctest.py
```

Then we would use the path `../readme.txt` in `test_doctest.py` to reference this file.

Alternatively, we can specify a package name and the path can be relative to that package like the following:

```
tests.addTests(doctest.DocFileSuite("readme.txt",
                               package="stock_alerter"))
```

# Setup and teardown

One of the problems with doctests is that we have to explicitly set up everything inside the docstring. For example, the following is the doctest for the `update` method that we wrote earlier:

```
>>> from datetime import datetime
>>> stock = Stock("GOOG")
>>> stock.update(datetime(2011, 10, 3), 10)
>>> stock.price
10
```

In the first line, we import the `datetime` module. This is incidental to the example and clutters it up, but we have to add it, otherwise we will get the following error:

```
Failed example:
    stock.update(datetime(2011, 10, 3), 10)
Exception raised:
```

```
Traceback (most recent call last):

    ...

NameError: name 'datetime' is not defined
```

Is there a way to avoid repetition of these lines? Yes, there is.

Both `DocFileSuite` and `DocTestSuite` take a `globs` parameter. This parameter takes a dictionary of items that are used for the globals of the doctests, from where they can be accessed by the examples. The following is how we would do this:

```
import doctest
from datetime import datetime
from stock_alerter import stock


def load_tests(loader, tests, pattern):
    tests.addTests(doctest.DocTestSuite(stock, globs={
        "datetime": datetime,
        "Stock": stock.Stock
    }))
    tests.addTests(doctest.DocFileSuite("readme.txt",
        package="stock_alerter"))
    return tests
```

> Note that we have to pass in not only the datetime module, but also the `Stock` class. By default, `doctest` uses the module's own globals in the execution context. This is why we were able to use the `Stock` class in our doctests so far. When we replace the execution context via the `globs` parameter, then we have to explicitly set the `Stock` object to be a part of the execution context.

`DocFileSuite` and `DocTestSuite` also take the `setUp` and `tearDown` parameters. These parameters take a function that will be called before and after each doctest. This is a good place to perform any setup or teardown of the environment that is needed by the test. The function has also passed a `DocTest` object, which can be used during setup and teardown. The `DocTest` object has many attributes, but the one most commonly used is the `globs` attribute. This is the dictionary of the execution context and it can be added to in the setup to instantiate objects that will be reused between objects. The following is an example of such a use:

```
import doctest
from datetime import datetime
```

```
from stock_alerter import stock


def setup_stock_doctest(doctest):
    s = stock.Stock("GOOG")
    doctest.globs.update({"stock": s})


def load_tests(loader, tests, pattern):
    tests.addTests(doctest.DocTestSuite(stock, globs={
        "datetime": datetime,
        "Stock": stock.Stock
    }, setUp=setup_stock_doctest))
    tests.addTests(doctest.DocFileSuite("readme.txt",
        package="stock_alerter"))
    return tests
```

By instantiating and passing in the stock to the doctests, we can remove the need to instantiate it in the individual tests, so the test was initially like the following:

```
def is_increasing_trend(self):
    """Returns True if the past three values have been strictly
    increasing

    Returns False if there have been less than three updates
    so far

    >>> stock = Stock("GOOG")
    >>> stock.is_increasing_trend()
    False
    """
```

Now the test becomes the following:

```
def is_increasing_trend(self):
    """Returns True if the past three values have been strictly
    increasing

    Returns False if there have been less than three updates
    so far

    >>> stock.is_increasing_trend()
```

```
False
"""
```

Why do we instantiate and pass in `stock` via the `setUp` function instead of using the `glob` parameter? The reason is because we want a new instance of `Stock` for each of the tests. Since `setUp` and `tearDown` are called before each test, a new instance of `stock` is added to `doctest.glob` each time.

# Limitations of doctest

The biggest limitation of `doctest` is that it only compares printed output. This means that any output that could be variable will lead to test failures. The following is an example:

```
>>> exchange
{'GOOG': <stock_alerter.stock.Stock object at 0x00000000031F8550>,
'AAPL': <stock_alerter.stock.Stock object at 0x00000000031F8588>}
```

This doctest has the potential to fail for two reasons:

- The order in which a dictionary object is printed out is not guaranteed by Python, which means it could be printed out in the opposite order, sometimes leading to failure
- The `Stock` object might be at a different address each time, so that part will fail to match the next time the test is run

The solution to the first problem is to ensure that the output is deterministic. For example, the following approach will work:

```
>>> for key in sorted(exchange.keys()):
...     print(key, exchange[key])
...
AAPL <stock_alerter.stock.Stock object at 0x00000000031F8550>
GOOG <stock_alerter.stock.Stock object at 0x00000000031F8588>
```

There is still the issue of the object address, though. To solve this, we need to use doctest directives.

# Doctest directives

doctest supports a number of directives that change the behavior of the module.

The first directive that we will look at is ELLIPSIS. This directive allows us to use three dots . . . to match any text. We can use this to match the object address, as in the following:

```
>>> for key in sorted(exchange.keys()): #doctest: +ELLIPSIS
...     print(key, exchange[key])
...
AAPL <stock_alerter.stock.Stock object at 0x0...>
GOOG <stock_alerter.stock.Stock object at 0x0...>
```

The example will now pass.

. . . will match whatever address is printed at runtime. We enable the directive by adding the comment #doctest: +ELLIPSIS to the example. This will turn on the directive for this example only. Subsequent examples in the same doctest will have it off unless it is specifically turned on for them.

Some other commonly used directives are:

- NORMALIZE_WHITESPACE: By default, doctest matches whitespace exactly. A space will not match with a tab, and newlines will not match unless they are at the exact same places. Sometimes, we might want to prettify the expected output by wrapping lines or indenting them so that they are easier to read. In such cases, the NORMALIZE_WHITESPACE directive can be set so that doctest will treat all counts of whitespace as equal.

- IGNORE_EXCEPTION_DETAIL: When matching exceptions, doctest looks at both the type of exception as well as the exception message. When this directive is enabled, only the type is checked for a match.

- SKIP: An example with this directive is skipped completely. This may be because the documentation is intentionally showing an example that doesn't work or one whose output is random. It can also be used to comment out doctests that aren't working.

- REPORT_ONLY_FIRST_FAILURE: doctest by default continues to execute subsequent examples after a failure, and will report failures in those as well. Many times, failure in one of the examples causes subsequent failures in following examples and can cause many error reports, making it harder to identify the first example to fail that caused all the other failures. This directive will only report the first failure.

This is not a comprehensive list of directives, but they cover the most commonly used ones.

Multiple directives can be given on separate lines or separated by commas. The following will work:

```
>>> for key in sorted(exchange.keys()):
...     print(key, exchange[key])
...     #doctest: +ELLIPSIS
...     #doctest: +NORMALIZE_WHITESPACE
AAPL      <stock_alerter.stock.Stock object at 0x0...>
GOOG      <stock_alerter.stock.Stock object at 0x0...>
```

Or, the following can also work:

```
>>> for key in sorted(exchange.keys()):
...     print(key, exchange[key])
...     #doctest: +ELLIPSIS, +NORMALIZE_WHITESPACE
AAPL      <stock_alerter.stock.Stock object at 0x0...>
GOOG      <stock_alerter.stock.Stock object at 0x0...>
```

Directives can also be passed via the optionflags parameter to DocFileSuite and DocTestSuite. The directives take effect for the entire file or module when passed in the following way:

```
options = doctest.ELLIPSIS | doctest.NORMALIZE_WHITESPACE
tests.addTests(doctest.DocFileSuite("readme.txt",
                                    package="stock_alerter",
                                    optionflags=options))
```

In the doctest, we can then turn off certain directives as needed, as shown in the following:

```
>>> for key in sorted(exchange.keys()):
...     print(key, exchange[key])
... #doctest: -NORMALIZE_WHITESPACE
AAPL <stock_alerter.stock.Stock object at 0x0...>
GOOG <stock_alerter.stock.Stock object at 0x0...>
```

Using directives is a good way to selectively enable or disable specific behavior on doctests.

# How do doctests fit into the TDD process?

Now that we have a pretty good idea of doctests, the next question is: how does this fit into the TDD process? Remember, in the TDD process, we write the test first, and then the implementation later. Do doctests fit in with this process?

In a way, yes. Doctests are not a particularly good fit for doing TDD for single methods. The unittest module is a better choice for those. Where doctest shines is at package-level interaction. Explanations interspersed with examples really bring out interaction between different modules and classes within the package. Such doctests can be written out at the beginning, giving a high-level overview of how we want the package as a whole to work. These tests will fail. As individual classes and methods are written, the tests will start to pass.

# Summary

In this chapter, you took a look at Python's doctest module. You saw how it helps you embed examples within docstrings. You looked at different ways to write doctests including method and package docstrings. You also looked at moving package level doctests into a separate file and running them. Maintaining doctests is important, and you looked at ways to maintain doctests better, using setup and teardown and including them in the regular test suite. Finally, you looked at some limitations and how you can use directives to overcome some of the limitations.

In the next chapter, you will get your first introduction to third-party tools with a look at the nose2 package.

# 8
# Extending unittest with nose2

So far we have been using the `unittest` test runner to run our tests. There are a number of other third-party test runners that have been created by the Python community. One of the most popular ones is nose2. nose2 provides additional features that improve on the default test runner.

## Getting started with nose2

Installing nose2 is a breeze. The easiest way to install it is via pip with the following command:

```
pip install nose2
```

Let us now run our tests using nose2. From the stock alerter project directory, run the `nose2` command (we might have to add it to the path first). nose2 has test autodiscovery by default, so just running the command should give the following output:

```
.........................................................
---------------------------------------------------------------------

Ran 63 tests in 0.109s


OK
```

As we can see, the `nose2` command gives the same output as `unittest`. nose2 which also discovered the same tests and ran them. By default, nose2 autodiscover patterns are compatible with `unittest`, so we can just drop in nose2 as a replacement runner without changing any code.

# Writing tests for nose2

Apart from picking up the existing tests written with the unittest module and running them, nose2 also supports new ways of writing tests.

To start with, nose2 allows tests to be regular functions. We don't need to create a class and inherit it from any base class. As long as the function starts with the word test, it is considered a test and executed.

We can take the following test:

```
class StockTest(unittest.TestCase):
    def setUp(self):
        self.goog = Stock("GOOG")


    def test_price_of_a_new_stock_class_should_be_None(self):
        self.assertIsNone(self.goog.price)
```

And write the above test as follows:

```
def test_price_of_a_new_stock_class_should_be_None():
    goog = Stock("GOOG")
    assert goog.price is None
```

As we can see, writing tests this way reduces some of the boilerplate code that we had to do before:

- We no longer have to create a class to hold the tests in
- We no longer have to inherit from any base class
- We don't even have to import the unittest module

We just write the tests as regular functions, and nose2 will autodiscover and run the tests.

Apart from moving the test to a regular function, there is one other change that we have made, and this is the way we are asserting on the expected result.

Previously, we did:

```
self.assertIsNone(self.goog.price)
```

When the test is a function, we do the following:

```
assert goog.price is None
```

Why this change? The `unittest.TestCase` class provides a lot of built-in assertion methods. When we inherit from this class, we can use those methods in our tests. When we write tests as a function, we no longer have access to those methods. Fortunately, nose2 supports Python's in-built `assert` statement, so we can just use that in our test.

The `assert` statement also supports taking a message parameter like the following:

```
assert goog.price is None, "Price of a new stock should be None"
```

If a test fails, the message will be printed to the output as follows:

```
======================================================================
FAIL: stock_alerter.tests.test_stock.FunctionTestCase (test_price_of_a_
new_stock_class_should_be_None)
----------------------------------------------------------------------
Traceback (most recent call last):
  ...
    assert goog.price is None, "Price of a new stock should be None"
AssertionError: Price of a new stock should be None


----------------------------------------------------------------------
```

# Setup and teardown

nose2 also supports setup and teardown for function-style test cases. This is done by setting the `setup` and `teardown` attributes on the *function object*. It works as follows:

```
def setup_test():
    global goog
    goog = Stock("GOOG")

def teardown_test():
    global goog
    goog = None

def test_price_of_a_new_stock_class_should_be_None():
    assert goog.price is None, "Price of a new stock should be None"

test_price_of_a_new_stock_class_should_be_None.setup = setup_test
test_price_of_a_new_stock_class_should_be_None.teardown = \
    teardown_test
```

Setup and teardown is limited with function-style tests in the sense that there is no way to pass state from the setup function to the test case and the teardown function. This is the reason why we have to declare that goog variable in the setup as global. This is the only way we can access it in the test case and the teardown function.

# Parameterized tests

nose2 also supports parameterized tests. Also called data-driven tests, these are nothing but running the same test with different combinations of data.

Take a look at the following three tests that we wrote earlier:

```
class StockTrendTest(unittest.TestCase):
    def setUp(self):
        self.goog = Stock("GOOG")

    def given_a_series_of_prices(self, prices):
        timestamps = [datetime(2014, 2, 10), datetime(2014, 2, 11),
                      datetime(2014, 2, 12), datetime(2014, 2, 13)]
        for timestamp, price in zip(timestamps, prices):
            self.goog.update(timestamp, price)

    def test_increasing_trend_true_if_
        price_increase_for_3_updates(self):
        self.given_a_series_of_prices([8, 10, 12])
        self.assertTrue(self.goog.is_increasing_trend())

    def test_increasing_trend_is_false_if_price_decreases(self):
        self.given_a_series_of_prices([8, 12, 10])
        self.assertFalse(self.goog.is_increasing_trend())

    def test_increasing_trend_is_false_if_price_equal(self):
        self.given_a_series_of_prices([8, 10, 10])
        self.assertFalse(self.goog.is_increasing_trend())
```

By parameterizing the test, we can write it like the following:

```
from nose2.tools.params import params


def given_a_series_of_prices(stock, prices):
```

```
    timestamps = [datetime(2014, 2, 10), datetime(2014, 2, 11),
                  datetime(2014, 2, 12), datetime(2014, 2, 13)]
    for timestamp, price in zip(timestamps, prices):
        stock.update(timestamp, price)


@params(
    ([8, 10, 12], True),
    ([8, 12, 10], False),
    ([8, 10, 10], False)
)
def test_stock_trends(prices, expected_output):
    goog = Stock("GOOG")
    given_a_series_of_prices(goog, prices)
    assert goog.is_increasing_trend() == expected_output
```

The `params` decorator allows us to specify a series of different inputs. The test is run once with each input. An input is a tuple where each element of the tuple is passed to the test function as a parameter. In the example above, the test will first be run with *prices=[8, 10, 12], expected_output=True*, then again with *prices=[8, 12, 10], expected_output=False*, and so on.

When a test fails, the output looks like the following:

```
======================================================================
FAIL: stock_alerter.tests.test_stock.test_stock_trends:2
[8, 12, 10], True
----------------------------------------------------------------------
Traceback (most recent call last):
  ...
    assert goog.is_increasing_trend() == expected_output
AssertionError


======================================================================
```

nose2 gives the parameter number that failed as :2 and underneath the exact data that was passed to the test.

Parameterized tests are a great way to reduce repetitive tests, where we are doing the same sequence of steps, with different data each time.

# Generated tests

Apart from parameterized tests, nose2 also supports generated tests. This is similar to parameterized tests. The difference is that parameterized tests have all the inputs hardcoded while writing the test, whereas they can be created at run time in generated tests.

The following is an example to clarify:

```
def test_trend_with_all_consecutive_values_upto_100():
    for i in range(100):
        yield stock_trends_with_consecutive_prices, [i, i+1, i+2]


def stock_trends_with_consecutive_prices(prices):
    goog = Stock("GOOG")
    given_a_series_of_prices(goog, prices)
    assert goog.is_increasing_trend()
```

When we run the above test, we see that a hundred tests have been run. What is going on here? Let us look at it in a little more detail.

Unlike a regular test function, this one yields a value, making it a generator function. The `yield` statement returns the function to be executed followed by the data to be passed to the function. Each time through the loop, the test function yields, and the yielded function is executed with the corresponding parameters. Since the loop runs a hundred times, a hundred tests are generated and executed.

When a test fails, the following output is shown:

```
======================================================================
FAIL: stock_alerter.tests.test_stock.test_trend_with_all_consecutive_
values_upto_100:100
[99, 100, 100]
----------------------------------------------------------------------
Traceback (most recent call last):
  ...
    assert goog.is_increasing_trend()
AssertionError


----------------------------------------------------------------------
```

Like with the parameterized tests, the output shows the test number that failed along with the exact inputs that were used to execute the test.

# Layers

If we look at the tests for our `Stock` class, we see that we have created three test classes: `StockTest`, `StockTrendTest`, and `StockCrossOverSignalTest`. All the three classes have some repetition in the `setUp` code, as shown in the following:

```
class StockTest(unittest.TestCase):
    def setUp(self):
        self.goog = Stock("GOOG")


class StockCrossOverSignalTest(unittest.TestCase):
    def setUp(self):
        self.goog = Stock("GOOG")
```

What if we could share part of the setup between them?

nose2 has another way to write tests called **Layers**. Layers allow us to organize our tests hierarchically. The following is an example of some of the `Stock` tests rewritten using Layers:

```
from nose2.tools import such


with such.A("Stock class") as it:

    @it.has_setup
    def setup():
        it.goog = Stock("GOOG")

    with it.having("a price method"):
        @it.has_setup
        def setup():
            it.goog.update(datetime(2014, 2, 12), price=10)

        @it.should("return the price")
        def test(case):
```

```
        assert it.goog.price == 10


    @it.should("return the latest price")
    def test(case):
        it.goog.update(datetime(2014, 2, 11), price=15)
        assert it.goog.price == 10


with it.having("a trend method"):
    @it.should("return True if last three updates were
        increasing")
    def test(case):
        it.goog.update(datetime(2014, 2, 11), price=12)
        it.goog.update(datetime(2014, 2, 12), price=13)
        it.goog.update(datetime(2014, 2, 13), price=14)
        assert it.goog.is_increasing_trend()


it.createTests(globals())
```

The entire syntax is new, so let us look at it carefully.

First, we need to import such. **Such** is the name of a domain specific language that makes it easy to write tests using nose2 layers. The following line imports it for us:

```
from nose2.tools import such
```

Next, we set up the top most layer as follows:

```
with such.A("Stock class") as it:
```

A layer can contain setup and teardown functions, test cases, and sub-layers. Such uses Python's context manager syntax to define a layer. We define the top topmost layer using the such.A method. It might sound strange to name a method as A, but the name has been chosen so that reading the line sounds natural to an English speaker. such.A takes a string as a parameter. This is just a descriptive string for the tests to follow.

The output of such.A is assigned to a variable. By convention it is called it, again the name being chosen so that the following usage will be like English sentences.

Having created the topmost layer, we then create the setup function for the layer, as shown in the following:

```
@it.has_setup
def setup():
    it.goog = Stock("GOOG")
```

The name of the function can be anything, we just need to mark it as the setup function by decorating it with the `has_setup` decorator. This decorator is a method of the `it` object, hence we write `@it.has_setup`. Similarly, we can use the `has_teardown` decorator to mark a function to be used for teardown.

In the `setup` function, we can store any stateful information as attributes of the `it` object. These can be referenced in sub-layers or in test cases.

Next, we create a sub-layer by calling the having method, as shown in the following:

```
with it.having("a price method"):
```

Again, this is a context manager, so we use it with the `with` statement. Unlike the top level layer, we don't need to assign it to any variable.

The sub-layer then defines its own setup function, as shown in the following:

```
@it.has_setup
def setup():
    it.goog.update(datetime(2014, 2, 12), price=10)
```

This `setup` function is called in addition to the setup function of the parent layer.

Next, we create a test case, as shown in the following:

```
@it.should("return the price")
def test(case):
    assert it.goog.price == 10
```

Test cases are marked using the `should` decorator. The decorator takes a description string which explains the test.

We continue with the same syntax to create another test, as shown in the following:

```
@it.should("return the latest price")
def test(case):
    it.goog.update(datetime(2014, 2, 11), price=15)
    assert it.goog.price == 10
```

That ends the sub-layer. Back in the top layer, we create a second sub-layer to hold the tests for the `is_increasing_trend` function, as shown in the following:

```
with it.having("a trend method"):
    @it.should("return True if last three updates were
        increasing")
    def test(case):
        it.goog.update(datetime(2014, 2, 11), price=12)
        it.goog.update(datetime(2014, 2, 12), price=13)
        it.goog.update(datetime(2014, 2, 13), price=14)
        assert it.goog.is_increasing_trend()
```

Finally, we call the `createTests` method to convert all this code into test cases, as shown in the following:

```
it.createTests(globals())
```

The `createTests` method should be called at the end of the topmost layer. It takes a single parameter of the current `globals`.

If the `createTests` method is not called, none of the tests will be executed.

Let us now run the tests. Layers is actually implemented as a nose2 plugin, so we need to use the following command to enable the plugin and run the tests:

```
nose2 --plugin nose2.plugins.layers
```

When we do this, the three tests written using Layers are executed along with all the other tests.

We can get nicer output by also enabling the Layer Reporter plugin with the following command:

```
nose2 --plugin nose2.plugins.layers --layer-reporter -v
```

We now get the output like the following:

```
A Stock class
  having a price method
    should return the price ... ok
    should return the latest price ... ok
  having a trend method
    should return True if last three updates were increasing ... ok
```

The descriptive strings that we gave for the Layers and tests are outputted here. When written well, the text should be readable as regular English sentences.

As we can see, Layers allow us to organize tests logically, sharing fixtures between parent and child. A layer can have any number of sub-layers and those, in turn, can contain further layers.

Let us quickly summarize what we have just learned:

- `such.A`: This is used as a context manager to create the topmost layer.
- `it.has_setup`: This is a decorator to mark a setup function for a layer.
- `it.has_teardown`: This is a decorator to mark a teardown function for a layer.
- `it.having`: This is used as a context manager to create a sub-layer.
- `it.should`: This is a decorator to mark a test case.
- `it.createTests`: This is a method that converts all the Layers code into test cases. Call it as the last line of code in the topmost layer, passing in `globals()`.

# nose2 plugins

In the previous section, we saw how we needed to enable the Layers plugin before we could run our layer tests. nose2 comes with a large set of plugins that enhance or extend its behavior. In fact, support for all the parameterized tests and generated tests that we saw earlier are actually implemented as nose2 plugins. The difference is that parameterized and generated tests are loaded by default, so we didn't need to explicitly enable them.

In this section, we'll take a look at some of the popular plugins. Keep in mind that there are many more plugins that we aren't going to discuss here.

# Doctest support

If we have not integrated doctests into the unittest framework as described in the previous chapter, then we can configure nose2 to autodiscover and run doctests.

Activate the plugin with the following command:

```
nose2 --plugin nose2.plugins.doctests --with-doctest
```

This will autodiscover and run doctests along with all the other kinds of tests.

# Writing test results to an XML file

nose2 has support for writing out test results into an XML file. Many tools can read this file format to understand the results of a test run. For example, continuous integration tools can find out if all the tests passed, and, if not, which tests failed.

Activate the plugin with the following command:

```
nose2 --plugin nose2.plugins.junitxml --junit-xml
```

This will create a file called `nose2-junit.xml` in the current directory. The file will contain something like the following:

```
<testsuite errors="0" failures="1" name="nose2-junit" skips="0"
tests="166" time="0.172">

  <testcase classname="stock_alerter.tests.test_action.EmailActionTest"
name="test_connection_closed_after_sending_mail" time="0.000000" />


  . . .


  <testcase classname="stock_alerter.tests.test_stock.having a trend
method" name="test 0000: should return True if the last three updates
were increasing" time="0.000000">

    <failure message="test failure">Traceback (most recent call last):
    File "...\src\stock_alerter\tests\test_stock.py", line 78, in test
      assert it.goog.is_increasing_trend()
AssertionError
    </failure>


  </testcase>
</testsuite>
```

The root element gives a summary of the entire test run, how many errors, failures, and skips there were, the number of tests, and the total time to run all the tests. Each child then summarizes a single test. If the test failed, then a traceback is included as well.

# Measuring test coverage

nose2 also supports measuring the test coverage. We can use this to identify if there are lines or branches of code that do not have tests, or which modules have poor test coverage.

Before we can use this plugin, we need to install some dependent packages with this command:

```
pip install nose2[coverage-plugin]
```

This will install two packages — cov-core and coverage — which are used by this plugin.

Once installed, we can enable the plugin with this command:

```
nose2 --with-coverage
```

Since this plugin is loaded by default, we don't need to give the --plugin parameter. Running the above command will give the following output:

```
----------- coverage: platform win32, python 3.4.0-final-0 -----------
Name                          Stmts   Miss  Cover
--------------------------------------------------
stock_alerter\__init__            3      3     0%
stock_alerter\action             18      8    56%
stock_alerter\alert              13      4    69%
stock_alerter\event               8      4    50%
stock_alerter\legacy             36     12    67%
stock_alerter\processor           8      0   100%
stock_alerter\reader             15      5    67%
stock_alerter\rule               33     12    64%
stock_alerter\stock              52     19    63%
```

The output above shows how many statements are in each module, how many are not covered by tests, and the percentage of coverage.

The plugin also creates a file called .coverage that stores the coverage results in binary form. This file can be used to get different kinds of reports. For example, we can use the following command to get HTML output:

```
nose2 --with-coverage --coverage-report html
```

The command will create a directory called `htmlcov`, which contains a set of files. If we open up `index.html` in a browser, then we get a fully interactive coverage report. We can click on any module and get details on exactly which lines were covered and which were not, as shown in the following screenshot:

# Coverage for **stock_alerter\action** : 56%

18 statements  |  10 run  |  8 missing  |  0 excluded

```
 1  import smtplib
 2  from email.mime.text import MIMEText
 3
 4
 5  class PrintAction:
 6      def execute(self, content):
 7          print(content)
 8
 9
10  class EmailAction:
11      """Send an email when a rule is matched"""
12      from_email = "alerts@stocks.com"
13
14      def __init__(self, to):
15          self.to_email = to
16
17      def execute(self, content):
18          message = MIMEText(content)
19          message["Subject"] = "New Stock Alert"
20          message["From"] = "alerts@stocks.com"
21          message["To"] = self.to_email
22          smtp = smtplib.SMTP("email.stocks.com")
23          try:
24              smtp.send_message(message)
25          finally:
26              smtp.quit()
```

*« index    coverage.py v3.7.1*

Other options for report types are `term` for terminal output, `term-missing` to also output the uncovered lines on the terminal, and `annotate`, which creates a copy of each of the source files with an annotation on whether the line was covered or not.

Multiple options can be combined like the following:

```
nose2 --with-coverage --coverage-report html --coverage-report term
```

# Debugging test failures

Another useful nose2 plugin is the debugger plugin. This plugin will activate the Python Debugger (pdb) when a test fails, allowing us to investigate why exactly the failure occurred.

Activate the plugin with the following command:

```
nose2 --plugin nose2.plugins.debugger --debugger
```

When a test fails, we drop into pdb and can use all the pdb commands to investigate the failure, as shown in the following:

```
F
> c:\python34\lib\unittest\case.py(787)_baseAssertEqual()
-> raise self.failureException(msg)
(Pdb) u
> c:\python34\lib\unittest\case.py(794)assertEqual()
-> assertion_func(first, second, msg=msg)
(Pdb) u
> c:\projects\tdd_with_python\src\stock_alerter\tests\test_stock.py(60)
test_stock_update()
-> self.assertEqual(100, self.goog.price)
(Pdb) self.goog.price
10
```

# nose2 configuration

Running the various plugins requires using many command line switches. For example, if we want to run coverage, as well as doctest and XML output, the command is as follows:

```
nose2 --with-coverage --coverage-report html --plugin nose2.plugins.
junitxml --junit-xml --plugin nose2.plugins.doctests --with-doctest
```

This is cumbersome, and if we want to run this combination by default, then it is very painful to keep repeating the parameters over and over.

To solve this problem, nose2 supports putting all configurations in to a configuration file. nose2 will then read the settings from the file, and we won't need to pass anything on the command line.

Create a file called nose2.cfg in the src directory with the following contents:

```
[unittest]
test-file-pattern=test_*.py
test-method-prefix=test
plugins = nose2.plugins.coverage
          nose2.plugins.junitxml
          nose2.plugins.layers
exclude-plugins = nose2.plugins.doctest

[layer-reporter]
always-on = False
colors = True

[junit-xml]
always-on = True
path = nose2.xml

[coverage]
always-on = False
coverage-report = ["html", "xml"]
```

Let us examine these contents.

nose2 uses the normal INI file syntax for its configuration. General configuration is put in the [unittest] section, while plugin specific options are under their own sections. Under each section, options are configured using key-value pairs.

We have configured the following above:

- **test-file-pattern**: This is the pattern to search for in the file name when identifying test files in autodiscovery.
- **test-method-prefix**: This is the prefix to search for to identify test case function and method names.
- **plugins**: These are the plugins to load by default. Put each plugin on a separate line, referring to the plugin module here. This is equivalent to the `--plugin` command line switch. Note that this only loads the plugin, and some plugins need to be explicitly turned on (for example, the `coverage` plugin).
- **exclude-plugin**: These are any plugins that need to be turned off. Usually, this is applied to plugins that are turned on by default (for example, parameterized or generated tests support).

We then configure the plugins. Each plugin has its own set of options. The one common option is as follows:

- **always-on**: Set to `True` if this plugin is turned on by default. For example, when the `JUnit` plugin is always on, every test run will create the XML file output. Otherwise, we have to use the `--junit-xml` switch on the command line to activate it.

nose2 also supports multiple configuration files. The `--config` switch can be used to specify which configuration file to use, as shown in the following:

```
nose2 --config <filename>
```

This way you can use the default configuration for developer options and create specific config files for continuous integration or other uses. For example, you might want junitxml and coverage to be always on when running under automated tools, but have them off when developers run the tests.

nose2 configuration files can also be checked into source control, so that all the developers use the same set of options.

# Summary

In this chapter, you looked at nose2, a powerful test runner and plugin suite, that extends the unittest framework. nose2 can be used as a drop-in replacement for the unittest test runner. It can also be used to extend unittest functionality with useful plugins. Finally, it can be used to write new types of tests such as function tests, parameterized tests, generated tests, and layer-based tests. nose2 also supports configuration files, so it can be run consistently between developers as well as integrating well with automation tools.

In the next chapter, you will take a look at some more advanced testing patterns.

# 9
# Unit Testing Patterns

Throughout this book, we have looked at various patterns and anti-patterns in TDD. In this chapter, you are going to take a look at some additional patterns that we haven't discussed before in this book. In the process of doing so, you will also take a look at some more advanced features provided by the Python `unittest` module, such as test loaders, test runners, and skipping tests.

## Pattern – fast tests

One of the key goals of TDD is to write tests that execute quickly. We will be running the tests often when doing TDD— possibly even every few minutes. The TDD habit is to run the tests multiple times when developing code, refactoring, before checkins, and before deployments. If tests run any longer, we will be reluctant to run them often, which defeats the purpose of the tests.

With that in mind, some techniques for keeping tests fast are as follows:

- **Disable unwanted external services**: Some services are not central to the purpose of the application and can be disabled. For instance, perhaps we use a service to collect analytics on how users use our application. Our application might be making a call to this service on every action. Such services can be disabled , enabling tests to run faster.

- **Mock out external services**: Other external services such as servers, databases, caches, and so on might be central to the functioning of the application. External services take time to start up, shut down, and communicate with. We want to mock these out and have our tests run against the mock.

- **Use fast variants of services**: If we must use a service, then make sure it is fast. For example, replace a database with an in-memory database, which is much faster and takes little time to start and shut down. Similarly, we can replace a call to an e-mail server with a fake in-memory e-mail server that just records the e-mails to be sent, without actually sending the e-mail.

- **Externalize configuration**: What does configuration have to do with unit testing? Simple: if we need to enable or disable services, or replace services with fake services, then we need to have different configurations for the regular application and for when running unit tests. This requires us to design the application in a way that allows us to easily switch between multiple configurations.

- **Run tests for the current module only**: Both the `unittest` test runner and third-party runners allow us to run a subset of tests—tests for a specific module, class, or even a single test. This is a great feature for large tests suites with thousands of tests, as it allows us to run just the tests for the module we are working on.

# Pattern – running a subset of tests

We already saw a simple way of running a subset of tests by simply specifying the module or test class on the command line, as shown in the following:

```
python -m unittest stock_alerter.tests.test_stock
```

```
python -m unittest stock_alerter.tests.test_stock.StockTest
```

This works for the common case of when we want to run a subset based on the module. What if we want to run tests based on some other parameter? Maybe we want to run a set of basic smoke tests, or we want to run only integration tests, or we want to skip tests when running on a specific platform or Python version.

The `unittest` module allows us to create test suites. A **test suite** is a collection of test classes that are run. By default, `unittest` performs an autodiscovery for tests and internally creates a test suite with all the tests that match the discovery pattern. However, we can also manually create different test suites and run them.

Test suites are created using the `unittest.TestSuite` class. The `TestSuite` class has the following two methods of interest:

- `addTest`: This method takes a `TestCase` or another `TestSuite` and adds it to the suite

- `addTests`: Similar to `addTest`, this method takes a list of `TestCase` or `TestSuite` and adds it to the suite

So, how do we use this function?

First, we write a function that makes the suite and returns it, as shown in the following:

```
def suite():
    test_suite = unittest.TestSuite()
    test_suite.addTest(StockTest("test_stock_update"))
    return test_suite
```

We can choose the specific tests that we want in the suite. We've added a single test to the suite over here.

Next, we need to write a script to run this suite, as shown in the following:

```
import unittest

from stock_alerter.tests import test_stock

if __name__ == "__main__":
    runner = unittest.TextTestRunner()
    runner.run(test_stock.suite())
```

Here, we create a `TextTestRunner` that will run the tests and pass it the suite or tests. `unittest.TextTestRunner` is a test runner that accepts a suite of tests and runs the suite, showing the results of the test, run on the console.

 unittest.TextTestRunner is the default test runner that we have been using so far. It is possible to write our own test runners. For example, we might write a custom test runner to implement a GUI interface, or one that writes test output into an XML file.

When we run this script, we get the following output:

```
.
-----------------------
Ran 1 test in 0.000s

OK
```

Similarly, we can create different suites for different subsets of tests—for example, a separate suite containing just integration tests—and run only specific suites as per our needs.

# Test loaders

One of the problems with the suite function is that we have to add each test individually into the suite. This is a cumbersome process if we have a lot of tests. Fortunately, we can simplify the process by using a `unittest.TestLoader` object to load a bunch of tests for us, as shown in the following:

```
def suite():
    loader = unittest.TestLoader()
    test_suite = unittest.TestSuite()
    test_suite.addTest(StockTest("test_stock_update"))
    test_suite.addTest(
        loader.loadTestsFromTestCase(StockCrossOverSignalTest))
    return test_suite
```

Here, the loader extracts all the tests from the `StockCrossOverSignalTest` class and creates a suite out of it. We can return the suite directly if that is all we want, or we can create a new suite with additional tests. In the example above, we create a suite containing a single test from the `StockTest` class and all the tests from the `StockCrossOverSignalTest` class.

`unittest.TestLoader` also contains some other methods for loading tests:

- `loadTestsFromModule`: This method takes a module and returns a suite of all the tests in that module.

- `loadTestsFromName`: This method takes a string reference to a module, class, or function and extracts the tests from there. If it is a function, the function is called and the test suite returned by the function is returned. The string reference is in dotted format, meaning we can pass in something like `stock_alerter.tests.test_stock` or `stock_alerter.tests.test_stock.StockTest`, or even `stock_alerter.tests.test_stock.suite`.

- `discover`: This method executes the default autodiscovery process and returns the collected tests as a suite. The method takes three parameters: the start directory, the pattern to find `test` module (default `test*.py`), and the top-level directory.

Using these methods, we can create test suites with just the tests that we want. We can create different suites for different purposes and execute them from the test script.

# Using the load_tests protocol

A simpler way to create test suites is with the `load_tests` function. As we saw in *Chapter 7, Executable Documentation with doctest,* the `unittest` framework calls the `load_tests` function if it is present in the test module. The function should return a `TestSuite` object containing the tests to be run. `load_tests` is a better solution when we want to just slightly modify the default autodiscovery process.

`load_tests` passes three parameters: the loader being used to load the tests, a suite of tests that are going to be loaded by default, and the test pattern that has been specified for the search.

Suppose we do not want to run the `StockCrossOverSignalTest` tests if the current platform is Windows. We can write a `load_tests` function like the following:

```python
def load_tests(loader, tests, pattern):
    suite = unittest.TestSuite()
    suite.addTest(loader.loadTestsFromTestCase(StockTest))
    if not sys.platform.startswith("win"):
        suite.addTest(
            loader.loadTestsFromTestCase(StockCrossOverSignalTest))
    return suite
```

Now the `StockCrossOverSignalTest` tests will be run only on non-windows platforms. When using the `load_tests` method, we don't need to write a separate script to run tests or create a test runner. It hooks into the autodiscovery process and is therefore much simpler to use.

# Skipping tests

In the previous section, we used the `load_tests` mechanism to skip some tests if the platform was Windows. The `unittest` module gives a simpler way to do the same using the `skip` decorator. Simply decorate a class or method with the decorator and the test will be skipped, as shown in the following:

```python
@unittest.skip("skip this test for now")
def test_stock_update(self):
    self.goog.update(datetime(2014, 2, 12), price=10)
    assert_that(self.goog.price, equal_to(10))
```

The decorator takes a parameter where we specify the reason that the test is being skipped. When we run all the tests, we get an output like the following:

```
...............................................s..
----------------------------------------------------------

Ran 59 tests in 0.094s


OK (skipped=1)
```

And when the tests are run in verbose mode, we get an output like the following:

```
test_stock_update (stock_alerter.tests.test_stock.StockTest) ... skipped
'skip this test for now'
```

The `skip` decorator skips a test unconditionally, but `unittest` provides two more decorators, `skipIf` and `skipUnless`, which allow us to specify a condition to skip the tests. These decorators take a `Boolean` value as the first parameter and a message as the second parameter. `skipIf` will skip the test if the `Boolean` is `True`, while `skipUnless` will skip the test if the `Boolean` is `False`.

The following test will run on all platforms except windows:

```
@unittest.skipIf(sys.platform.startswith("win"), "skip on windows")
def test_stock_price_should_give_the_latest_price(self):
    self.goog.update(datetime(2014, 2, 12), price=10)
    self.goog.update(datetime(2014, 2, 13), price=8.4)
    self.assertAlmostEqual(8.4, self.goog.price, delta=0.0001)
```

While the following test will run only on windows:

```
@unittest.skipUnless(sys.platform.startswith("win"),
    "only run on windows")
def test_price_is_the_latest_even_if_updates_are_made_out_of_order(self):
    self.goog.update(datetime(2014, 2, 13), price=8)
    self.goog.update(datetime(2014, 2, 12), price=10)
    self.assertEqual(8, self.goog.price)
```

The `skip`, `skipIf`, and `skipUnless` decorators can be used on test methods as well as test classes. When applied to classes, all the tests in the class are skipped.

# Pattern – using attributes

The `nose2` test runner has a useful `attrib` plugin that allows us to set attributes on test cases and select tests that match particular attributes.

For example, the following test has three attributes set:

```
def test_stock_update(self):
    self.goog.update(datetime(2014, 2, 12), price=10)
    self.assertEqual(10, self.goog.price)


test_stock_update.slow = True
test_stock_update.integration = True
test_stock_update.python = ["2.6", "3.4"]
```

When nose2 is run via the following command, then the plugin is enabled, and only the tests that have the integration attribute set to `True` are executed:

```
nose2 --plugin=nose2.plugins.attrib -A "integration"
```

The plugin can also run all tests that have a specific value in a list. Take the following command:

```
nose2 --plugin=nose2.plugins.attrib -A "python=2.6"
```

The preceding command will run all tests that have the `python` attribute set to `2.6` or containing the value `2.6` in a list. It will select and run the `test_stock_update` test, shown previously.

The plugin can also run all tests that *do not* have an attribute set. Take the following command:

```
nose2 --plugin=nose2.plugins.attrib -A "!slow"
```

The preceding command will run all tests that are not marked as slow.

The plugin can also take complex conditions, so we can give the following command:

```
nose2 --plugin=nose2.plugins.attrib -E "integration and '2.6' in python"
```

This test runs all the tests that have the `integration` attribute, as well as `2.6` in the `python` attribute list. Note that we used the `-E` switch to specify that we are giving a `python` condition expression.

The attribute plugin is a great way to run specific subsets of tests without having to manually make test suites out of each and every combination that we might want to run.

# Attributes with vanilla unittests

The `attrib` plugin requires nose2 to work. What if we are using the regular `unittest` module? The design of the `unittest` module allows us to easily write a simplified version in just a few lines of code, as shown in the following:

```python
import unittest


class AttribLoader(unittest.TestLoader):
    def __init__(self, attrib):
        self.attrib = attrib

    def loadTestsFromModule(self, module, use_load_tests=False):
        return super().loadTestsFromModule(module,
            use_load_tests=False)

    def getTestCaseNames(self, testCaseClass):
        test_names = super().getTestCaseNames(testCaseClass)
        filtered_test_names = [test
                        for test in test_names
                        if hasattr(getattr(testCaseClass,
                            test), self.attrib)]
        return filtered_test_names


if __name__ == "__main__":
    loader = AttribLoader("slow")
    test_suite = loader.discover(".")
    runner = unittest.TextTestRunner()
    runner.run(test_suite)
```

This little piece of code will only run those tests that have the `integration` attribute set on the test function. Let us look a little deeper into the code.

First, we subclass the default `unittest.TestLoader` class and create our own loader called `AttribLoader`. Remember, the **loader** is the class responsible for loading the tests from a class or module.

Next, we override the `getTestCaseNames` method. This method returns a list of test case names from a class. Here, we call the parent method to get the default list of tests, and then select those test function that have the required attribute. This filtered list is returned, and it is only these tests that will be executed.

So why have we overridden the `loadTestsFromModule` method as well? Well, simple: the default behavior for loading tests is to match by the `test` prefix on the method, but if the `load_tests` function is present, then everything is delegated to the `load_tests` function. Therefore, all modules that have the `load_tests` function defined will take priority over our attribute filtering scheme.

When using our loader, we call the default implementation, but set the `use_load_tests` parameter to `False`. This means that none of the `load_tests` functions will be executed, and the tests to be loaded will be determined only by the filtered list that we return. If we would like to give priority to `load_tests` (as is the default behavior), then we just need to remove this method from `AttribLoader`.

Okay, now that the loader is ready, we then modify our test running script to use this loader, instead of the default loader. We get the loaded test suite by calling the `discover` method, which, in turn, calls our overridden `getTestCaseNames`. We pass this suite to the runner and run the tests.

The loader can be easily modified to support selecting tests that *don't* have a given attribute or to support more complex conditionals. We can then add support to the script to accept the attribute on the command line and pass it on to the loader.

# Pattern – expected failures

Sometimes, we have tests that are failing, but, for whatever reason, we don't want to fix it yet. It could be that we found a bug and wrote a failing test that demonstrates the bug (a very good practice), but we have decided to fix the bug later. Now, the whole test suite is failing.

On one hand, we don't want the suite to fail because we know this bug and want to fix it later. On the other hand, we don't want to remove the test from the suite because it reminds us that we need to fix the bug. What do we do?

Python's `unittest` module provides a solution: marking tests as expected failures. We can do this by applying the `unittest.expectedFailure` decorator to the test. The following is an example of it in action:

```
class AlertTest(unittest.TestCase):

    @unittest.expectedFailure
    def test_action_is_executed_when_rule_matches(self):
```

```
goog = mock.MagicMock(spec=Stock)
goog.updated = Event()
goog.update.side_effect = \
    lambda date, value: goog.updated.fire(self)
exchange = {"GOOG": goog}
rule = mock.MagicMock(spec=PriceRule)
rule.matches.return_value = True
rule.depends_on.return_value = {"GOOG"}
action = mock.MagicMock()
alert = Alert("sample alert", rule, action)
alert.connect(exchange)
exchange["GOOG"].update(datetime(2014, 2, 10), 11)
action.execute.assert_called_with("sample alerts")
```

We get the following output when the tests are executed:

```
......x.................................................
--------------------------------------------------------
Ran 59 tests in 0.188s


OK (expected failures=1)
```

And the following is the verbose output:

```
test_action_is_executed_when_rule_matches (stock_alerter.tests.test_
alert.AlertTest) ... expected failure
```

# Pattern – data-driven tests

We briefly explored data-driven tests earlier. Data-driven tests reduce the amount of boilerplate test code by allowing us to write a single test execution flow and run it with different combinations of data.

The following is an example using the nose2 parameterization plugin that we looked at earlier in this book:

```
from nose2.tools.params import params


def given_a_series_of_prices(stock, prices):
    timestamps = [datetime(2014, 2, 10), datetime(2014, 2, 11),
                datetime(2014, 2, 12), datetime(2014, 2, 13)]
```

```
    for timestamp, price in zip(timestamps, prices):
        stock.update(timestamp, price)


@params(
    ([8, 10, 12], True),
    ([8, 12, 10], False),
    ([8, 10, 10], False)
)
def test_stock_trends(prices, expected_output):
    goog = Stock("GOOG")
    given_a_series_of_prices(goog, prices)
    assert goog.is_increasing_trend() == expected_output
```

Running tests like this requires the use of nose2. Is there a way to do something similar using the regular `unittest` module? For a long time there was no way to do this without resorting to metaclasses, but a new feature added with Python 3.4 has made this possible.

This new feature is the `unittest.subTest` context manager. All the code within the context manager block will be treated as a separate test, and any failures are reported independently. The following is an example:

```
class StockTrendTest(unittest.TestCase):
    def given_a_series_of_prices(self, stock, prices):
        timestamps = [datetime(2014, 2, 10), datetime(2014, 2, 11),
                      datetime(2014, 2, 12), datetime(2014, 2, 13)]
        for timestamp, price in zip(timestamps, prices):
            stock.update(timestamp, price)


    def test_stock_trends(self):
        dataset = [
            ([8, 10, 12], True),
            ([8, 12, 10], False),
            ([8, 10, 10], False)
        ]
        for data in dataset:
            prices, output = data
```

```
        with self.subTest(prices=prices, output=output):
            goog = Stock("GOOG")
            self.given_a_series_of_prices(goog, prices)
            self.assertEqual(output, goog.is_increasing_trend())
```

In this example, the test loops through the different scenarios and asserts each one. The whole Arrange-Act-Assert pattern occurs inside the subTest context manager. The context manager takes any keyword arguments as parameters and these are used in displaying error messages.

When we run the test, we get an output like the following:

```
.
------------------------

Ran 1 test in 0.000s


OK
```

As we can see, the whole test is considered a single test and it shows that the test passed.

Suppose we change the test to make it fail in two of the three cases, as shown in the following:

```
class StockTrendTest(unittest.TestCase):
    def given_a_series_of_prices(self, stock, prices):
        timestamps = [datetime(2014, 2, 10), datetime(2014, 2, 11),
                      datetime(2014, 2, 12), datetime(2014, 2, 13)]
        for timestamp, price in zip(timestamps, prices):
            stock.update(timestamp, price)

    def test_stock_trends(self):
        dataset = [
            ([8, 10, 12], True),
            ([8, 12, 10], True),
            ([8, 10, 10], True)
        ]
        for data in dataset:
            prices, output = data
            with self.subTest(prices=prices, output=output):
```

```
        goog = Stock("GOOG")
        self.given_a_series_of_prices(goog, prices)
        self.assertEqual(output, goog.is_increasing_trend())
```

Then, the output becomes as follows:

```
======================================================================
FAIL: test_stock_trends (stock_alerter.tests.test_stock.StockTrendTest)
(output=True, prices=[8, 12, 10])
----------------------------------------------------------------------
Traceback (most recent call last):
  File "c:\Projects\tdd_with_python\src\stock_alerter\tests\test_stock.
py", line 78, in test_stock_trends
    self.assertEqual(output, goog.is_increasing_trend())
AssertionError: True != False


======================================================================
FAIL: test_stock_trends (stock_alerter.tests.test_stock.StockTrendTest)
(output=True, prices=[8, 10, 10])
----------------------------------------------------------------------
Traceback (most recent call last):
  File "c:\Projects\tdd_with_python\src\stock_alerter\tests\test_stock.
py", line 78, in test_stock_trends
    self.assertEqual(output, goog.is_increasing_trend())
AssertionError: True != False


----------------------------------------------------------------------
Ran 1 test in 0.000s


FAILED (failures=2)
```

As we can see in the preceding output, it shows a single test was run, but each failure is reported individually. In addition, the values that were used when the test failed are appended to the end of the test name, making it easy to see exactly which condition failed. The values displayed here are the parameters that were passed into the subTest context manager.

# Pattern – integration and system tests

Throughout this book, we've stressed the fact that unit tests are not integration tests. They have a different purpose to validating that the system works when integrated. Having said that, integration tests are also important and shouldn't be ignored. Integration tests can be written using the same `unittest` framework that we use for writing unit tests. The key points to keep in mind when writing integration tests are as follows:

- **Still disable non-core services**: Keep non-core services such as analytics or logging disabled. These do not affect the functionality of the application.

- **Enable all core services**: Every other service should be live. We don't want to mock or fake these because this defeats the whole purpose of an integration test.

- **Use attributes to tag integration tests**: By doing this, we can easily select only the unit tests to run during development, while enabling integration tests to be run during continuous integration or before deployment.

- **Try to minimize setup and teardown time**: For example, don't start and stop a server for each and every test. Instead, use module or package level fixtures to start and stop a service once for the entire set of tests. When doing this, we have to be careful that our tests do not mess up the state of the service in-between tests. In particular, a failing test or a test error should not leave the service in an inconsistent state.

# Pattern – spies

Mocks allow us to replace an object or class with a dummy mock object. We've seen how we can then make the mock return predefined values, so that the class under test doesn't even know that it has made a call to a mock object. However, sometimes we might want to just record that the call was made to an object, but allow the execution flow to continue to the real object and return. Such an object is known as a **spy**. A spy retains the functionality of recording calls and being able to assert on the calls afterwards, but it does not replace a real object like a regular mock does.

The `wraps` parameter when creating a `mock.Mock` object allows us to create spy behavior in our code. It takes an object as a value, and all calls to the mock are forwarded to the object we pass, and the return value is sent back to the caller. The following is an example:

```
def test_action_doesnt_fire_if_rule_doesnt_match(self):
    goog = Stock("GOOG")
    exchange = {"GOOG": goog}
```

```
rule = PriceRule("GOOG", lambda stock: stock.price > 10)
rule_spy = mock.MagicMock(wraps=rule)
action = mock.MagicMock()
alert = Alert("sample alert", rule_spy, action)
alert.connect(exchange)
alert.check_rule(goog)
rule_spy.matches.assert_called_with(exchange)
self.assertFalse(action.execute.called)
```

In the above example, we are creating a spy for the `rule` object. The spy is nothing but a regular mock object that wraps the real object, as specified in the `wraps` parameter. We then pass the spy to the alert. When `alert.check_rule` is executed, the method called the `matches` method on the spy. The spy records the call details, and then forwards the call to the real rule object and returns the value from the real object. We can then assert on the spy to validate the call.

Spies are typically used when we would like to avoid over-mocking and use a real object, but we also would like to assert on specific calls. They are also used when it is difficult to calculate mock return values by hand, and it is better to just do the real calculation and return the value.

# Pattern – asserting a sequence of calls

Sometimes, we want to assert that a particular sequence of calls occurred across multiple objects. Consider the following test case:

```
def test_action_fires_when_rule_matches(self):
    goog = Stock("GOOG")
    exchange = {"GOOG": goog}
    rule = mock.MagicMock()
    rule.matches.return_value = True
    rule.depends_on.return_value = {"GOOG"}
    action = mock.MagicMock()
    alert = Alert("sample alert", rule, action)
    alert.connect(exchange)
    goog.update(datetime(2014, 5, 14), 11)
    rule.matches.assert_called_with(exchange)
    self.assertTrue(action.execute.called)
```

In this test, we are asserting that a call was made to the `rule.matches` method as well as a call being made to the `action.execute` method. The way we have written the assertions does not check the order of these two calls. This test will still pass even if the `matches` method is called after the `execute` method. What if we want to specifically check that the call to the `matches` method happened before the call to the `execute` method?

Before answering this question, let us take a look at this interactive Python session. First, we create a mock object, as follows:

```
>>> from unittest import mock
>>> obj = mock.Mock()
```

Then, we get two child objects that are attributes of the mock, as follows:

```
>>> child_obj1 = obj.child1
>>> child_obj2 = obj.child2
```

Mock objects by default return new mocks whenever an attribute is accessed that doesn't have a `return_value` configured. So `child_obj1` and `child_obj2` will also be mock objects.

Next, we call some methods on our mock objects, as follows:

```
>>> child_obj1.method1()
<Mock name='mock.child1.method1()' id='56161448'>
>>> child_obj2.method1()
<Mock name='mock.child2.method1()' id='56161672'>
>>> child_obj2.method2()
<Mock name='mock.child2.method2()' id='56162008'>
>>> obj.method()
<Mock name='mock.method()' id='56162232'>
```

Again, no `return_value` is configured, so the default behavior for the method call is to return new mock objects. We can ignore those for this example.

Now, let us look at the `mock_calls` attribute for the child objects. This attribute contains a list of all the recorded calls on the mock object, as shown in the following:

```
>>> child_obj1.mock_calls
[call.method1()]
>>> child_obj2.mock_calls
[call.method1(), call.method2()]
```

The mock objects have the appropriate method calls recorded, as expected. Let us now take a look at the attribute on the main `obj` mock object, as follows:

```
>>> obj.mock_calls
[call.child1.method1(),
 call.child2.method1(),
 call.child2.method2(),
 call.method()]
```

Now, this is surprising! The main mock object seems to not only have details of its own calls, but also all the calls made by the child mocks!

So, how can we use this feature in our test to assert the order of the calls made across different mocks?

Well, what if we wrote the above test like the following:

```
def test_action_fires_when_rule_matches(self):
    goog = Stock("GOOG")
    exchange = {"GOOG": goog}
    main_mock = mock.MagicMock()
    rule = main_mock.rule
    rule.matches.return_value = True
    rule.depends_on.return_value = {"GOOG"}
    action = main_mock.action
    alert = Alert("sample alert", rule, action)
    alert.connect(exchange)
    goog.update(datetime(2014, 5, 14), 11)
    main_mock.assert_has_calls(
        [mock.call.rule.matches(exchange),
         mock.call.action.execute("sample alert")])
```

Here, we create a main mock object called `main_mock`, and the `rule` and `action` mocks are child mocks of this. We then use the mocks as usual. The difference is that we use `main_mock` in the assert section. Since `main_mock` has a record of the order in which calls are made to the child mocks, this assertion can check the order of calls to the `rule` and `action` mocks.

Let us go a step further. The `assert_has_calls` method only asserts that the calls were made and that they were in that particular order. The method *does not* guarantee that these were the *only* calls made. There could have been other calls before the first call or after the last call, or even in-between the two calls. The assertion will pass as long as the calls we are asserting were made, and that between them the order was maintained.

To strictly match the calls, we can simply do an `assertEqual` on the `mock_calls` attribute like the following:

```python
def test_action_fires_when_rule_matches(self):
    goog = Stock("GOOG")
    exchange = {"GOOG": goog}
    main_mock = mock.MagicMock()
    rule = main_mock.rule
    rule.matches.return_value = True
    rule.depends_on.return_value = {"GOOG"}
    action = main_mock.action
    alert = Alert("sample alert", rule, action)
    alert.connect(exchange)
    goog.update(datetime(2014, 5, 14), 11)
    self.assertEqual([mock.call.rule.depends_on(),
                      mock.call.rule.matches(exchange),
                      mock.call.action.execute("sample alert")],
                     main_mock.mock_calls)
```

In the above, we assert the `mock_calls` with a list of expected calls. The list must match exactly—no missing calls, no extra calls, nothing different. The thing to be careful about is that we must list out *every* call. There is a call to `rule.depends_on`, which is done in the `alert.connect` method. We have to specify that call, even though it is not related to the functionality we are trying to test.

Usually, matching every call will lead to verbose tests as all calls that are tangential to the functionality being tested also need to be put in the expected output. It also leads to brittle tests as even slight change in calls elsewhere, which might not lead to change in behavior in this particular test, will still cause the test to fail. This is why the default behavior for `assert_has_calls` is to only determine whether the expected calls are present, instead of checking for an exact match of calls. In the rare cases where an exact match is required, we can always assert on the `mock_calls` attribute directly.

# Pattern – patching the open function

One of the most common cases of mocking is to mock out file access. This is actually a little cumbersome because the open function can be used in a number of different ways. It can be used as a regular function or as a context manager. The data can be read using many methods such as read, readlines, and so on. In turn, some of these functions, return iterators that can be iterated upon. It is a pain to sit and mock all these out in order to be able to use them in tests.

Fortunately, the mocking library provides an extremely helpful mock_open function, which returns a mock that handles all these situations. Let us see how we can use this function.

The following is the code for a FileReader:

```
class FileReader:
    """Reads a series of stock updates from a file"""
    def __init__(self, filename):
        self.filename = filename


    def get_updates(self):
        """Returns the next update everytime the method is called"""


        with open(self.filename, "r") as fp:
            for line in fp:
                symbol, time, price = line.split(",")
                yield (symbol, datetime.strptime(time,
                    "%Y-%m-%dT%H:%M:%S.%f"), int(price))
```

This class reads stock updates from a file and returns each update, one by one. The method is a generator, and uses the yield keyword to return updates, one at a time.

**A quick primer on generators**

**Generators** are functions that use a `yield` statement instead of a `return` statement to return values. Each time the generator is executed, the execution does not start at the beginning of the function, but instead continues running from the previous `yield` statement. In the example above, when the generator is executed, it parses the first line of the file, then yields the value. The next time it is executed, it continues once more through the loop and returns the second value, then the third value, and so on until the loop is over. Each execution of the generator returns one stock update. For more on generators, check out the Python documentation or online articles. One such article can be found at `http://www.jeffknupp.com/blog/2013/04/07/improve-your-python-yield-and-generators-explained/`.

In order to test the `get_update` method, we will need to create different kinds of file data and verify that the method reads them properly and returns values as expected. In order to do this, we will mock out the open function. The following is one such test:

```
class FileReaderTest(unittest.TestCase):
    @mock.patch("builtins.open",
                mock.mock_open(read_data="""\
        GOOG,2014-02-11T14:10:22.13,10"""))
    def test_FileReader_returns_the_file_contents(self):
        reader = FileReader("stocks.txt")
        updater = reader.get_updates()
        update = next(updater)
        self.assertEqual(("GOOG",
                        datetime(2014, 2, 11, 14, 10, 22, 130000),
                        10), update)
```

In the above test, we are starting with patching the `builtins.open` function. The `patch` decorator can take a second parameter, in which we can specify the mock object to be used after patching. We call the `mock.mock_open` function to create an appropriate mock object, which we pass to the `patch` decorator.

The `mock_open` function takes a `read_data` parameter, in which we can specify what data should be returned when the mocked file is read. We use this parameter to specify the file data we want to test against.

The rest of the test is fairly simple. The only thing to note is in the following line:

```
updater = reader.get_updates()
```

Since get_updates is a generator function, a call to the get_updates method does not actually return a stock update, but instead returns the generator object. This generator object is stored in the updater variable. We use the built-in next function to get the stock update from the generator and assert that it is as expected.

# Pattern – mocking with mutable args

One gotcha that can bite us is when arguments to mocked out objects are mutable. Take a look at the following example:

```
>>> from unittest import mock
>>> param = ["abc"]
>>> obj = mock.Mock()
>>> _ = obj(param)
>>> param[0] = "123"

>>> obj.assert_called_with(["abc"])
Traceback (most recent call last):
  File "<stdin>", line 1, in <module>
  File "C:\Python34\lib\unittest\mock.py", line 760, in assert_called_with
    raise AssertionError(_error_message()) from cause
AssertionError: Expected call: mock(['abc'])
Actual call: mock(['123'])
```

Whoa! What happened there? The error says the following:

```
AssertionError: Expected call: mock(['abc'])
Actual call: mock(['123'])
```

Actual call was mock(['123'])? But we called the mock as follows:

```
>>> param = ["abc"]
>>> obj = mock.Mock()
>>> _ = obj(param)
```

It's pretty clear that we called it with ["abc"]. So why is this failing?

The answer is that the mock object only stores a reference to the call arguments. So, when the line param[0] = "123" was executed, it affected the value that was saved as the call argument in the mock. In the assertion, it looks at the saved call argument, and sees that the call was made with the data ["123"], so the assertion fails.

The obvious question is: why is it that the mock stores a reference to the parameters? Why doesn't it make a copy of the arguments so that the stored copy doesn't get changed if the object passed as a parameter is changed later on? The answer is that making a copy creates a new object, so all assertions where object identity is compared in the argument list will fail.

So what do we do now? How do we make this test work?

Simple: we just inherit from `Mock` or `MagicMock` and change the behavior to make a copy of the arguments, as shown in the following:

```
>>> from copy import deepcopy
>>>
>>> class CopyingMock(mock.MagicMock):
...         def __call__(self, *args, **kwargs):
...             args = deepcopy(args)
...             kwargs = deepcopy(kwargs)
...             return super().__call__(*args, **kwargs)
```

This mock just makes a copy of the arguments and then invokes the default behavior passing in the copy.

The assertion now passes, as shown in the following:

```
>>> param = ["abc"]
>>> obj = CopyingMock()
>>> _ = obj(param)
>>> param[0] = "123"
>>> obj.assert_called_with(["abc"])
```

Keep in mind that when we use `CopyingMock`, we cannot use any object identity comparisons with the arguments as they will now fail, as shown in the following:

```
>>> class MyObj:
...         pass
...
>>> param = MyObj()
>>> obj = CopyingMock()
>>> _ = obj(param)

>>> obj.assert_called_with(param)
Traceback (most recent call last):
```

```
    File "<stdin>", line 1, in <module>
    File "C:\Python34\lib\unittest\mock.py", line 760, in assert_called_
with
        raise AssertionError(_error_message()) from cause
AssertionError: Expected call: mock(<__main__.MyObj object at
0x00000000026BAB70>)
Actual call: mock(<__main__.MyObj object at 0x00000000026A8E10>)
```

# Summary

In this chapter, you looked at some other patterns for unit testing. You looked at how to speed up tests and how you can run specific subsets of tests. You looked at various patterns for running subset of tests, including creating your own test suites and using the `load_tests` protocol. You saw how to use the nose2 attrib plugin to run a subset of tests based on test attributes and how to implement that functionality with the default unit test runner. We then examined features for skipping tests and marking tests as expected failures. You finally looked at how we could write data-driven tests.

Next, we moved on to some mocking patterns, starting with how to implement spy functionality. You also looked at the problem of validating a sequence of mock calls across multiple mocks. You then looked at the `mock_open` function to help us easily mock filesystem access, and in the process you took a peek at how to work with generator functions. Finally, you looked at the problem of using mocks when the arguments are mutable.

The next chapter is the final chapter in this book, where you will look at other tools that we can use in our TDD practice.

# 10
# Tools to Improve
# Test-Driven Development

Up to this point, we have mostly been looking at how to write and run tests. In this chapter, we will turn our attention to integrating the tests with the wider development environment. Having tests integrated into the development environment is important because it allows us to set up an automated process through which tests are executed regularly. We will also look at other tools that can improve the way we do TDD—from other test runners to libraries that make asserting easier.

## TDD tools

We looked at the nose2 test runner earlier in this book. Python has other popular third-party test runners. Python also has a number of libraries to make assertions more flexible and readable. These libraries can be used with both `unittest` compatible tests and the function style tests supported by third-party test runners. Let us take a look at some of these TDD tools.

### py.test

Like nose2, py.test is another popular third-party test runner. py.test supports many features like the following:

- Writing tests as ordinary functions.
- Using Python's `assert` statement to perform asserts.
- Ability to skip tests or mark tests as expected failures.
- Fixtures with setup and teardown support.

- Extensible plugin framework, with plugins available to do popular functionality such as XML output, coverage reporting, and running tests in parallel across multiple processors or cores.

- Tag tests with attributes.

- Integration with popular tools.

One of py.test's most unique features is funcargs. Take a look at the following code:

```python
import pytest


@pytest.fixture
def goog():
    return Stock("GOOG")


def test_stock_update(goog):
    assert goog.price is None
```

In this code, the `test_stock_update` function takes a parameter called `goog`. Additionally, we have a function called `goog`, which is marked with the `pytest.fixture` decorator. PyTest will match these two, call the appropriate fixture, and pass in the return value as a parameter to the test.

This solves the following two problems:

- It enables us to pass fixture values to function style test cases without having to resort to globals.

- Instead of writing a large fixture, we can create many small ones, and the test cases only use the fixtures that they need. This makes it easier to read test cases as we don't have to look at a large fixture setup that has different lines of setup meant for different tests.

The above example only scratches the surface of funcargs. `py.test` supports a number of other usage scenarios with funcargs. Definitely check out this popular test runner.

## py.test versus nose2

There isn't a lot to choose between nose2 and py.test. nose2 has a unique feature in writing tests using layers, while py.test has a unique feature in funcargs. Apart from that, both support running of `unittest` test cases, both have a robust plugin framework, and both can be integrated with all the tools we discuss in this chapter. The decision between them really comes down to a personal choice between layers versus funcargs, or if one supports a particular plugin that we really want. Definitely take a look at py.test at its homepage at `http://pytest.org/latest/`.

# Trial

Trial is a unit test runner that was originally built for testing Python's Twisted framework. Trial supports running vanilla unit tests written using the `unittest` module, as well as advanced features specifically for supporting applications based on network programming—clients, servers, and the like. The most important of these is support for asynchronous programming models, where a method might return immediately, but the actual return value is received later on. This is usually done using a concept called `Deferred`. Since this is a deep and niche topic, we won't go into a detailed discussion in this book. Just keep in mind that if you are doing anything with network programming, event-based systems, or asynchronous programming, then you should check out Trial at its homepage at `http://twistedmatrix.com/trac/wiki/TwistedTrial`.

# Sure

Sure is a Python library to help write assertions that are easier to read. It is a Python port of the should.js JavaScript library.

With Sure, we can take the following test:

```
def test_stock_update(self):
    """An update should set the price on the stock object

    We will be  using the `datetime` module for the timestamp
    """
    self.goog.update(datetime(2014, 2, 12), price=10)
    self.assertEqual(10, self.goog.price)
```

And, rewrite it to look like the following:

```
def test_stock_update(self):
    self.goog.update(datetime(2014, 2, 12), price=10)
    self.goog.price.should.equal(10)
```

 Notice how the assert has been replaced with a statement that reads like regular English. Sure adds a bunch of attributes to all objects to allow us to write asserts like this.

The following is how our float test would look like in Sure:

```
def test_stock_price_should_give_the_latest_price(self):
    self.goog.update(datetime(2014, 2, 12), price=10)
    self.goog.update(datetime(2014, 2, 13), price=8.4)
    self.goog.price.should.equal(8.4, epsilon=0.0001)
```

And, the following is how we would check for expected exceptions:

```
def test_negative_price_should_throw_ValueError(self):
    self.goog.update.when.called_with(datetime(2014, 2, 13), -1).\
        should.throw(ValueError)
```

Sure also supports using Python's `assert` statement as follows:

```
def test_stock_update(self):
    self.goog.update(datetime(2014, 2, 12), price=10)
    assert self.goog.price.should.equal(10)
```

Sure supports a large number of expressions like the one above to express a multitude of assertion conditions.

Sure uses some monkey patching to add these attributes to all objects. The monkey patching is done once the `import sure` statement is executed. For this reason, be careful to use Sure only on unit test files and not in any production file.

Monkey patching can be disabled by setting the SURE_DISABLE_NEW_SYNTAX environment variable to true before running tests. When monkey patching is disabled, Sure supports an alternate syntax using the expect function as follows:

```
def test_stock_price_should_give_the_latest_price(self):
    self.goog.update(datetime(2014, 2, 12), price=10)
    self.goog.update(datetime(2014, 2, 13), price=8.4)
    expect(self.goog.price).should.equal(8.4, epsilon=0.0001)
```

Full details on all available methods and syntax are available on the Sure homepage at http://falcao.it/sure/intro.html.

Since assertions are plain functions, we can use this library even when writing function style tests supported by nose2 and py.test.

# PyHamcrest

PyHamcrest is a Python port of the Java Hamcrest library. This is another library to enable us to write cleaner and more flexible asserts.

PyHamcrest defines its own `assert_that` function and a number of matchers such as `equal_to`. Using them, we can write a test like the following:

```python
def test_stock_update(self):
    self.goog.update(datetime(2014, 2, 12), price=10)
    assert_that(self.goog.price, equal_to(10))
```

PyHamcrest also has a system for writing custom matchers by inheriting from the `BaseMatcher` class. The following is a custom matcher that checks whether a stock has the crossover signal returning a particular value:

```python
class StockCrossoverMatcher(BaseMatcher):
    signal_names = {
        StockSignal.buy: "buy",
        StockSignal.sell: "sell",
        StockSignal.neutral: "neutral"
    }

    def __init__(self, signal, date_to_check):
        self.signal = signal
        self.date_to_check = date_to_check

    def _matches(self, item):
        return self.signal == \
            item.get_crossover_signal(self.date_to_check)

    def describe_to(self, description):
        signal_name = self.signal_names[self.signal]
        return description.append_text(
                "stock crossover signal is {} ".format(signal_name))
```

The class defines two methods: `_matches` and `describe_to`.

The `_matches` method takes the first parameter for the `assert_that` function call and returns whether it matches the given condition or not. In this case, we call the `get_crossover_signal` method and check whether it matches the signal that we were expecting.

The `describe_to` method returns a text description that is used for the message displayed when the assertion fails.

We also define a convenience function `is_buy_on`, which returns a matcher to match the `StockSignal.buy` signal as follows:

```
def is_buy_on(date_to_check):
    return StockCrossoverMatcher(StockSignal.buy, date_to_check)
```

With this, we can write a test like the following:

```
def test_with_upward_crossover_returns_buy(self):
    self.given_a_series_of_prices([
        29, 28, 27, 26, 25, 24, 23, 22, 21, 20, 46])
    assert_that(self.goog, is_buy_on(datetime(2014, 2, 13)))
```

Like Sure, PyHamcrest assertions are plain functions and are suitable for use in function style tests supported by nose2 and py.test. You can visit PyHamcrest's homepage at `https://github.com/hamcrest/PyHamcrest`.

# Integrating with build tools

It just takes a single line to execute our test cases. Then why would we want to integrate with build tools? Build tools support pre-requisites, so by integrating with such tools, we can ensure the tests are run before performing a critical task. An example would be to run all the tests before deploying the code to production.

## Paver

Paver is a popular Python-based build tool. It is built around the concept of tasks. Tasks are a sequence of commands that perform a particular action, such as building the application or running unit tests. Tasks are coded in regular Python and placed in a file called `pavement.py` in the project root.

We want to create a task that will run our unit tests. The following is how we can do that in Paver:

```
import subprocess
from paver.easy import task, consume_args, options, needs


@task
@consume_args
def test():
    args = []
    if hasattr(options, "args"):
        args = options.args
    p = subprocess.Popen(["python", "-m", "unittest"] + args)
    p.wait()
    return p.returncode
```

The task above simply runs a command to execute the `unittest` module. We use the `@consume_args` decorator, which tells Paver to take all the command line parameters and pass it to this task.

To run this Paver task, we simply execute the following on the command line:

**paver test -t . -s stock_alerter**

If we are using nose2, then we can modify the task as follows:

```
import subprocess
from paver.easy import task, consume_args, options, needs


@task
@consume_args
def test():
    args = []
    if hasattr(options, "args"):
        args = options.args
    p = subprocess.Popen(["nose2"] + args)
    p.wait()
    return p.returncode
```

Once we have the task, then we can use it in other tasks like the following:

```
@needs("test")
def deploy():
    # put the deployment commands here
    pass
```

This will run the `test` task every time the `deploy` task is executed. Only if the tests pass will the deployment of the code take place.

# Integrating with packaging tools

Packaging refers to how Python packages are generally distributed to users. Unless we are writing proprietary commercial software, we will want to distribute the unit tests along with the code and allow the end user to run the tests and verify that everything is working.

Packaging tools have been one of the most confusing parts of the Python ecosystem. There have been a number of different frameworks that, at different points, have been "the right way" to do things. As this book is being written, setuptools is the recommended way to package Python modules, so let us take a look at that first.

## Setuptools

Setuptools supports a test command for running the test suite. All we need to do is to configure it. We do this by specifying the `test_suite` parameter in `setup.py` as follows:

```
from setuptools import setup, find_packages

setup(
    name="StockAlerter",
    version="0.1",
    packages=find_packages(),
    test_suite="stock_alerter.tests",
)
```

When we do this, setuptools will pick up and run all the tests with the following command:

```
python setup.py test
```

The configuration above will only run the `unittest` compatible tests. We can't run any nose2 tests nor can we use nose2 plugins. Fortunately, nose2 also supports integration with setuptools. The `nose2.collector.collector` function returns a compatible test suite which setuptools can run. The following test suite executes all the tests found by nose2:

```
from setuptools import setup, find_packages


setup(
    name="StockAlerter",
    version="0.1",
    packages=find_packages(),
    tests_require=["nose2"],
    test_suite="nose2.collector.collector",
```

The `tests_require` parameter can be set to the packages that are required for running tests. We put `nose2` here, so even if the end user doesn't have nose2 installed, setuptools will install it for us before running the tests. If we use any third-party nose2 plugins, we can add those to the list here.

We can't pass any parameters when running tests this way. All configuration needs to be done in `nose2.cfg`. If there are some special settings that we would like to use only with the `setuptools` test command, we can put those in a special `setup.cfg` file. The settings in this file are used only when the nose tests are run via setuptools.

To integrate py.test with setuptools, we need to use the `cmdclass` technique that we use in the `distutils` integration in the following.

# Distutils

Python comes bundled with its own packaging system called **distutils**. Although setuptools is the preferred way, we might sometimes want to stick with distutils because it is bundled in the standard library.

Distutils supports adding custom commands to setup.py. We're going to use that feature to add a command that will run our tests. The following is what it looks like:

```
import subprocess
from distutils.core import setup, Command


class TestCommand(Command):
```

```
    user_options = []

    def initialize_options(self):
        pass

    def finalize_options(self):
        pass

    def run(self):
        p = subprocess.Popen(["python", "-m", "unittest"])
        p.wait()
        raise SystemExit(p.returncode)

setup(
    name="StockAlerter",
    version="0.1",
    cmdclass={
        "test": TestCommand
    }
)
```

The cmdclass option allows us to pass in a dict containing command names mapped to a command class. We configure the test command and map it to our TestCommand class.

The TestCommand class inherits from distutil's Command class. The Command class is an abstract base class; subclasses will need to create the user_options list as well as implement three methods: initialize_options, finalize_options, and run. We don't need to do anything in the first two methods, so we keep them empty.

The only method we need for our command is the run method. This method is called by distutils when the command is to be executed, and our implementation simply runs the shell command and returns the appropriate exit value.

The same technique can be used to run the nose2 tests or py.test tests as well.

# Integrating with continuous integration tools

Continuous integration tools allow us to validate the integrity of our application by running the test suite on every commit. We can configure them to raise an alert if any of the tests are failing, or even if the test coverage level drops too low.

## Jenkins

Jenkins is a popular Java-based continuous integration system. Integrating with Jenkins requires the nose2 runner because we will need to get output in an XML format.

The first thing we need to do is to configure Jenkins to run the unit tests as a part of the build. To do this, we add a shell step to the build and enter the command to run the tests. We need to enable the JUnit XML plugin and get coverage in XML format, as shown in the following screenshot:

We then need to tell Jenkins where to find the unit test results. Select the **Publish JUnit test result report** checkbox and enter the location of the nose2 unit test XML file, as shown in the following screenshot:

Enable the **Publish Cobertura Coverage Report** and select the location of the coverage XML output file, as shown in the following screenshot. The plugin also allows us to set alert limits for Line coverage. This will fail the build if coverage levels drop below the threshold specified here.

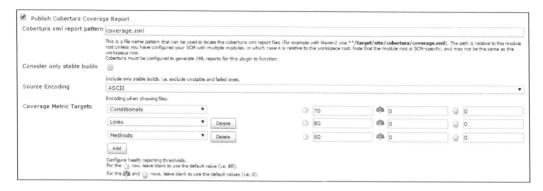

Once the configuration is done, Jenkins will run tests on every build, and give us a nice trend report of the unit tests as well as coverage statistics, as shown in the following screenshot:

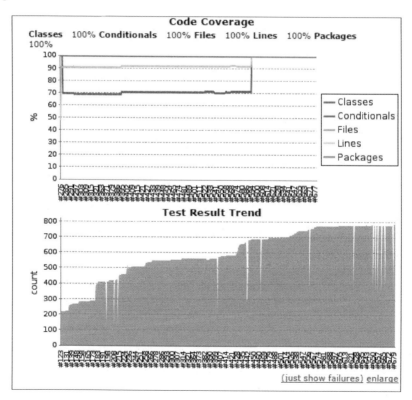

We can also dig in deeper to see details about specific suites or tests from within Jenkins, as shown in the following screenshot:

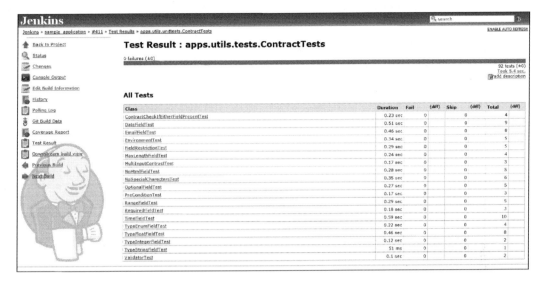

# Travis CI

Travis CI is the hot new kid on the block, becoming very popular in the Python community for open source packages, as shown in the following screenshot:

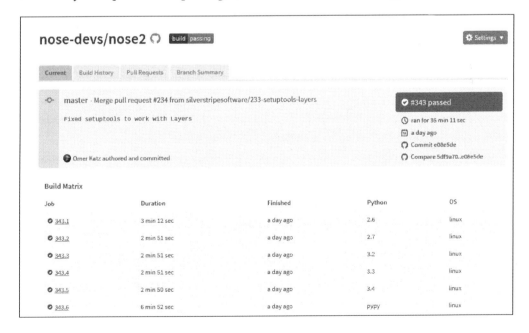

As a hosted service, it doesn't require any installation. Configuring Travis to run our unit tests is a breeze. All we need to do is to add the command to run the tests into the `script` section of the `.travis.yml` configuration file as follows:

```
script:
    - python -m unittest
```

or if we are using nose2:

```
script:
    - nose2
```

That's it. Now Travis will execute the command with every commit and let us know if the tests fail for any reason.

# Other tools

## tox

tox is a framework for maintaining a Python package across multiple versions of Python. For example, we can easily test that everything is working in Python 2.6 and Python 3.4. It works by creating virtual environments for each version and then running the unit tests under that environment.

 tox uses the virtualenv tool for creating virtual environments. This tool is bundled in the standard library with Python 3.4 and can be installed from PyPi for older version of Python. We don't cover this tool in this book, but if you aren't using it already, then do take a look at it.

A typical tox configuration file looks like the following:

```
[tox]
envlist = py33,py34

[testenv:py34]
deps = nose2
       sure
       pyhamcrest
```

```
commands = nose2


[testenv:py33]
deps = enum34
       sure
       pyhamcrest
commands = python -m unittest
```

The configuration includes the list of Python versions to test against. Each environment can have its own dependencies installed that we require to run the tests as well as the command required to run the tests. This command can be the vanilla `unittest` command, or a third-party runner such as nose2 or py.test.

When tox is executed, it creates a virtual environment for each of the Python versions, installs the required dependencies, and runs our tests in that environment. tox can be integrated with continuous integration systems so that compatibility is maintained with each commit.

# Sphinx

Sphinx is a documentation framework commonly used with Python projects. Sphinx supports embedding snippets of code examples within the documentation. Sphinx also has `sphinx.ext.doctest` plugin that can extract these code examples as doctests and run them to ensure that the documentation doesn't break.

The `sphinx.ext.doctest` plugin supports doctest fixtures for setup and teardown, and doctest options. Sphinx with the doctest plugin is a good option when our application requires a full-blown documentation system.

# IDE integration

We haven't talked about IDE integration yet. This is because most of the popular Python IDEs have built-in support for running unit tests from within the IDE. It is almost a basic feature these days. In addition, there are plugins available for popular text editors such as vim, emacs, and Sublime Text 3. We won't cover each and every one of these since they are too numerous. It only takes a quick online search to get the configuration or plugins we need to run tests from within our favorite IDE or text editor.

# Summary

In this chapter, you looked at some popular third-party tools to help us improve our TDD practice. Some of the tools such as `py.test` and `trial` are test runners with some unique features. Others such as `sure` and `pyhamcrest` are libraries that help us write cleaner tests. You looked at how we can integrate our unit tests into the wider development process: from putting them into the build environment and integrating with continuous integration tools, to enabling the `test` command when packaging our code. We then took a look at how we can maintain a package against multiple versions of Python and integrating tests into Sphinx so that our documentation doesn't break.

# A
# Answers to Exercises

This Appendix contains answers to the exercises presented throughout this book. Keep in mind that there is no single correct solution for any of these exercises. There are many possible solutions, each with their own advantages and disadvantages. Wherever possible, I have mentioned why I took a certain path, so that you can see my reasoning and compare the pros and cons with the solution that you have come up with.

## Red-Green-Refactor – The TDD Cycle

This exercise asks us to add support for updates which come out of order, that is, a newer update is followed by an older update. We need to use the timestamp to determine which update is newer and which is older.

The following is a test case for this requirement:

```
def test_price_is_the_latest_even_if_
    updates_are_made_out_of_order(self):
    self.goog.update(datetime(2014, 2, 13), price=8)
    self.goog.update(datetime(2014, 2, 12), price=10)
    self.assertEqual(8, self.goog.price)
```

In the test above, we first give the update for February 13, followed by the update for February 12. We then assert that the price attribute returns the latest price (for February 13). The test fails of course.

In order to make this test pass, we can't simply add the latest update to the end of the `price_history` list. We need to check the timestamp and insert it accordingly into the list, keeping it sorted by timestamp.

The `bisect` module provided in the Python standard library contains the `insort_left` function that inserts into a sorted list. We can use this function as follows (remember to import bisect at the top of the file):

```
def update(self, timestamp, price):
    if price < 0:
        raise ValueError("price should not be negative")
    bisect.insort_left(self.price_history, (timestamp, price))
```

In order to have a sorted list, the `price_history` list needs to keep a list of tuples, with the timestamp as the first element. This will keep the list sorted by the timestamp. When we make this change, it breaks our other methods that expect the list to contain the price alone. We need to modify them as follows:

```
@property
def price(self):
    return self.price_history[-1][1] \
        if self.price_history else None


def is_increasing_trend(self):
    return self.price_history[-3][1] < \
        self.price_history[-2][1] < self.price_history[-1][1]
```

With the above changes, all our existing tests as well as the new test start passing.

Now that we have the tests passing, we can look at refactoring the code to make it easier to read. Since the `price_history` list now contains tuples, we have to refer to the price element by tuple index, leading to statements list `price_history[-1][1]`, which are not very clear. We can make this clearer by using a named tuple that allows us to assign names to the tuple values. Our refactored Stock class now looks like the following:

```
PriceEvent = collections.namedtuple("PriceEvent",
    ["timestamp", "price"])


class Stock:
    def __init__(self, symbol):
        self.symbol = symbol
        self.price_history = []


    @property
    def price(self):
```

```
        return self.price_history[-1].price \
            if self.price_history else None


    def update(self, timestamp, price):
        if price < 0:
            raise ValueError("price should not be negative")
        bisect.insert_left(self.price_history, PriceEvent(timestamp,
price))


    def is_increasing_trend(self):
        return self.price_history[-3].price < \
            self.price_history[-2].price < \
                self.price_history[-1].price
```

After the change, we run the tests to ensure that everything still works.

# Code Smells and Refactoring

This exercise asks us to refactor the `Stock` class and extract all the moving average related calculations into a new class.

The following is the code that we start with:

```
def get_crossover_signal(self, on_date):
    NUM_DAYS = self.LONG_TERM_TIMESPAN + 1
    closing_price_list = \
        self.history.get_closing_price_list(on_date, NUM_DAYS)


    if len(closing_price_list) < NUM_DAYS:
        return StockSignal.neutral


    long_term_series = \
        closing_price_list[-self.LONG_TERM_TIMESPAN:]
    prev_long_term_series = \
        closing_price_list[-self.LONG_TERM_TIMESPAN-1:-1]
    short_term_series = \
        closing_price_list[-self.SHORT_TERM_TIMESPAN:]
    prev_short_term_series = \
```

```
            closing_price_list[-self.SHORT_TERM_TIMESPAN-1:-1]


    long_term_ma = sum([update.value
                        for update in long_term_series])\
                /self.LONG_TERM_TIMESPAN
    prev_long_term_ma = sum([update.value
                             for update in prev_long_term_series])\
                /self.LONG_TERM_TIMESPAN
    short_term_ma = sum([update.value
                         for update in short_term_series])\
                /self.SHORT_TERM_TIMESPAN
    prev_short_term_ma = sum([update.value
                              for update in prev_short_term_series])\
                /self.SHORT_TERM_TIMESPAN


    if self._is_crossover_below_to_above(prev_short_term_ma,
                                         prev_long_term_ma,
                                         short_term_ma,
                                         long_term_ma):
            return StockSignal.buy

    if self._is_crossover_below_to_above(prev_long_term_ma,
                                         prev_short_term_ma,
                                         long_term_ma,
                                         short_term_ma):
            return StockSignal.sell


    return StockSignal.neutral
```

As we can see, there are a number of calculations relating to identifying the moving average window and then calculating the moving average value. These calculations really deserve to be in their own class.

To start with, we create an empty MovingAverage class as follows:

```
class MovingAverage:
    pass
```

Now we need to make a design decision on how we want this class to be used. Let us decide that the class should take an underlying timeseries and should be able to compute the moving average at any point based on that timeseries. With this design, the class needs to take the timeseries and the duration of the moving average as parameters, as shown in the following:

```
def __init__(self, series, timespan):
    self.series = series
    self.timespan = timespan
```

We can now extract the moving average calculation into this class as follows:

```
class MovingAverage:
    def __init__(self, series, timespan):
        self.series = series
        self.timespan = timespan


    def value_on(self, end_date):
        moving_average_range = self.series.get_closing_price_list(
                                  end_date, self.timespan)
        if len(moving_average_range) < self.timespan:
            raise NotEnoughDataException("Not enough data")
        price_list = [item.value for item in moving_average_range]
        return sum(price_list)/len(price_list)
```

This is the same moving average calculation code from `Stock.get_signal_crossover`. The only notable point is that an exception is raised if there is not enough data to perform the calculation. Let us define this exception in the `timeseries.py` file as follows:

```
class NotEnoughDataException(Exception):
    pass
```

We can now use this method in `Stock.get_signal_crossover` as follows:

```
def get_crossover_signal(self, on_date):
    prev_date = on_date - timedelta(1)
    long_term_ma = \
        MovingAverage(self.history, self.LONG_TERM_TIMESPAN)
    short_term_ma = \
```

```
            MovingAverage(self.history, self.SHORT_TERM_TIMESPAN)


        try:
            long_term_ma_value = long_term_ma.value_on(on_date)
            prev_long_term_ma_value = long_term_ma.value_on(prev_date)
            short_term_ma_value = short_term_ma.value_on(on_date)
            prev_short_term_ma_value = short_term_ma.value_on(prev_date)
        except NotEnoughDataException:
            return StockSignal.neutral


        if self._is_crossover_below_to_above(prev_short_term_ma_value,
                                             prev_long_term_ma_value,
                                             short_term_ma_value,
                                             long_term_ma_value):
                return StockSignal.buy


        if self._is_crossover_below_to_above(prev_long_term_ma_value,
                                             prev_short_term_ma_value,
                                             long_term_ma_value,
                                             short_term_ma_value):
                return StockSignal.sell


        return StockSignal.neutral
```

Run the tests, and all 21 tests should pass.

Once we extract the calculation to a class, we find that the temporary variables that we created during *Replace Calculation with Temporary Variable* section in *Chapter 3, Code Smells and Refactoring* are not really required. The code is equally self-explanatory without them, so we can now get rid of them, as shown in the following:

```
def get_crossover_signal(self, on_date):
    prev_date = on_date - timedelta(1)
    long_term_ma = \
        MovingAverage(self.history, self.LONG_TERM_TIMESPAN)
    short_term_ma = \
```

```
        MovingAverage(self.history, self.SHORT_TERM_TIMESPAN)


    try:
        if self._is_crossover_below_to_above(
                short_term_ma.value_on(prev_date),
                long_term_ma.value_on(prev_date),
                short_term_ma.value_on(on_date),
                long_term_ma.value_on(on_date)):
            return StockSignal.buy


        if self._is_crossover_below_to_above(
                long_term_ma.value_on(prev_date),
                short_term_ma.value_on(prev_date),
                long_term_ma.value_on(on_date),
                short_term_ma.value_on(on_date)):
            return StockSignal.sell
    except NotEnoughDataException:
        return StockSignal.neutral


    return StockSignal.neutral
```

A final cleanup: now that we have moving average classes, we can replace the parameters to the _is_crossover_below_to_above method to take the moving average class instead of the individual values. The method now becomes as follows:

```
def _is_crossover_below_to_above(self, on_date, ma, reference_ma):
    prev_date = on_date - timedelta(1)
    return (ma.value_on(prev_date)
                < reference_ma.value_on(prev_date)
            and ma.value_on(on_date)
                > reference_ma.value_on(on_date))
```

And we can change the get_crossover_signal method to call this with the new parameters as follows:

```
def get_crossover_signal(self, on_date):
    long_term_ma = \
        MovingAverage(self.history, self.LONG_TERM_TIMESPAN)
    short_term_ma = \
```

```
        MovingAverage(self.history, self.SHORT_TERM_TIMESPAN)

    try:
        if self._is_crossover_below_to_above(
                on_date,
                short_term_ma,
                long_term_ma):
            return StockSignal.buy

        if self._is_crossover_below_to_above(
                on_date,
                long_term_ma,
                short_term_ma):
            return StockSignal.sell
    except NotEnoughDataException:
        return StockSignal.neutral

    return StockSignal.neutral
```

With this, our Extract Class refactoring is complete.

The get_crossover_signal class is now extremely easy to read and understand.

Notice how the design for the MovingAverage class builds on top of the TimeSeries class that we extracted earlier. As we refactor code and extract classes, we often find that the many classes get reused in other contexts. This is the advantage of having small classes with a single responsibility.

The refactoring into a separate class also allowed us to remove the temporary variables that we had created earlier, and made the parameters for the crossover condition much simpler. Again, these are side effects of having small classes with single responsibilities.

# B
# Working with Older Python Versions

This book has been written for Python 3.4. The version of `unittest` that comes with the Python 2.x standard library is an older version that doesn't support all the features that we discussed in this book. Additionally, the `mock` library was only made a part of the standard library from Python 3.3 onward.

Fortunately, all the features present in the newer versions of Python have been backported under the `unittest2` library. We can install this version from PyPi with the following command:

```
pip install unittest2
```

Once installed, we have to use the `unittest2` library in all references like the following:

```
import unittest2


class StockTest(unittest2.TestCase):

    ...
```

With these changes, we will be able to use all the features that we have been discussing in this book in all versions from Python 2.5 onward.

The same goes for the mocking library as well. The `mock` library was only added to the standard library with Python 3.3. The current mock library has been backported and is also available from PyPi. We can install it with the following command:

```
pip install mock
```

And we import it with the following command:

```
import mock
```

We can then use all the mocking goodness discussed in this book with earlier versions of Python as well.

# Writing code that is compatible across versions

Many Python modules these days are designed to run under multiple Python versions, especially supporting Python 2.x as well as Python 3.x versions. We will want to run the same tests in both versions, and to do this, we will need to write our code in such a way that the tests are compatible with both the versions.

Python's import mechanism gives us the flexibility we need to do this. At the top of the file, we import unittest like the following:

```
try:
    import unittest2 as unittest
except ImportError:
    import unittest
```

What this does is to first try and import unittest2. If we are running Python 2.x, then we should have installed this already. If it succeeds, then the module is imported and the module reference is renamed to unittest.

If we get an ImportError, then we are running Python 3.x, in which case we can import the unittest module bundled in the standard library.

Later in the code, we can just reference the unittest module and it will work normally.

This mechanism depends on the unittest2 module being always installed when using Python 2.x version. This is easily achieved by putting the unittest2 module as a dependency for only Python 2.x in our pip requirements file.

A similar approach works for mocks as follows:

```
try:
    from unittest import mock
except ImportError:
    import mock
```

Here we first try to import the `mock` library provided as a part of the `unittest` standard library module. This is available in Python 3.3 onward. If the import succeeds, then the mock library is imported. If it fails, it means that we are running an older Python version, so we directly import the `mock` library that we installed from PyPi.

Note how we use the line `from unittest import mock` instead of `import unittest.mock`. This is so that we end up with the same module reference name in both the cases. Once the import is done, we can reference the `mock` module in our code and it will work across Python versions.

# Running tests from the command line

Throughout the book, we have used the following syntax to run our tests:

```
python.exe -m unittest
```

The ability to directly run a module with the `-m` flag was only introduced with Python 2.7. This syntax will not work if we are using an older version of Python. Instead, the `unittest2` module from PyPi contains a `unit2` script that mimics this behavior. The command line parameters remain the same, so we get the following the command:

```
python3 -m unittest discover -s stock_alerter -t .
```

And the above command now becomes:

```
unit2 discover -s stock_alerter -t .
```

If we use a build tool, it becomes fairly simple to check the version of Python and execute the appropriate command, thereby allowing the developer to run the tests in a uniform way, irrespective of the Python version being used.

With these changes in place, we will be able to use all the features described in this book, while being able to support Python 2.x and Python 3.x uniformly.

# Running the examples in this book

The code examples in this book have been written for Python 3.4. They use some syntax that is not available in older versions of Python. Therefore, there are a few places we will need to change the code if we want to run the examples in, say, Python 2.6.

 The entire source code with all the changes below is available online at https://github.com/siddhi/test_driven_python. Get this code if you would like to run the example code in this book under Python 2.6, 2.7, 3.0, 3.1, 3.2, or 3.3

The following changes are required:

- Enum: The Enum library is not in the standard library with older Python versions. It has been backported and can be installed from PyPi. Install the Enum34 library to use this feature.

- set syntax: Newer versions of Python support the single curly braces shorthand syntax to create set objects like{"MSFT"}. In older versions, we will need to explicitly create sets with this equivalent longhand syntax: set(["MSFT"]).

- print statement: print is defined as a statement in Python 2.x, so we cannot call it as a function, neither can we mock it out. We can get around this by adding the line from __future__ import print_function to the top of all the files that use print.

- builtins: The builtins module is called __builtin__ in Python 2.x. Therefore, we need to use __builtin__.print or __builtin__.open when we want to mock the print or open functions.

- yield from expression: This expression is not available in older Python versions. It has to be replaced with an iteration.

- mock_open: This mock helper only mocks the read method in the backported version. It doesn't support mocking iteration on the file object. So, we need to change the implementation to not use iteration.

With these changes, the examples in this book will work on Python 2.6 onward.

# Index

## L

**Layers  171-175**
**legacy code**
  about  99, 100
  characterization tests  102
  characterization tests, writing  103
  example  100, 101
  pdb, using  104, 105
  Python interactive shell, using  102
  refactoring  119-121
**load_tests protocol**
  using  187
**long-term refactoring  122**

## M

**matchers**
  using  141, 142
**methods**
  patching  88-92
**mock library**
  installing  231
**mocks**
  best solutions  86, 87
  example  93-97
  versus fakes  87
  versus spies  87
  versus stubs  87
  writing  72-75
**Move Method to Class refactoring  63-67**
**msg parameter  23**
**mutable args**
  mocking with  203, 204

## N

**naming conventions  129**
**nose2**
  about  165
  configuration  179, 180
  generated tests, writing  170, 171
  installing  165
  Layers  171-175
  parameterized tests, writing  168, 169
  plugins  175

setup function, implementing  167
teardown function, implementing  167
tests, writing  166
versus py.test  209

## O

**objects**
  mocking  77-82
**open function**
  patching  201, 202
**organization, tests**
  about  126
  filesystem layout  127, 128
  naming convention  129
  test suite, grouping  130

## P

**package level doctests  153-155**
**packaging tools**
  integrating with  214
  setuptools  214, 215
**parameterized tests**
  writing, in nose2  168, 169
**patching**
  about  88
  considerations  92, 93
**Paver  212-214**
**pdb**
  commands  105
  implementing  106-109
  using  104, 105
**plugins, nose2**
  about  175
  doctests, running  175
  nose2 configuration  179, 180
  test coverage, measuring  177-179
  test failures, debugging  179
  test results, writing to XML file  176
**PyHamcrest**
  about  211, 212
  URL  212
**py.test**
  about  207, 208
  features  207, 208

## Thank you for buying
# Test-Driven Python Development

# About Packt Publishing

Packt, pronounced 'packed', published its first book, *Mastering phpMyAdmin for Effective MySQL Management*, in April 2004, and subsequently continued to specialize in publishing highly focused books on specific technologies and solutions.

Our books and publications share the experiences of your fellow IT professionals in adapting and customizing today's systems, applications, and frameworks. Our solution-based books give you the knowledge and power to customize the software and technologies you're using to get the job done. Packt books are more specific and less general than the IT books you have seen in the past. Our unique business model allows us to bring you more focused information, giving you more of what you need to know, and less of what you don't.

Packt is a modern yet unique publishing company that focuses on producing quality, cutting-edge books for communities of developers, administrators, and newbies alike. For more information, please visit our website at www.packtpub.com.

# About Packt Open Source

In 2010, Packt launched two new brands, Packt Open Source and Packt Enterprise, in order to continue its focus on specialization. This book is part of the Packt Open Source brand, home to books published on software built around open source licenses, and offering information to anybody from advanced developers to budding web designers. The Open Source brand also runs Packt's Open Source Royalty Scheme, by which Packt gives a royalty to each open source project about whose software a book is sold.

# Writing for Packt

We welcome all inquiries from people who are interested in authoring. Book proposals should be sent to author@packtpub.com. If your book idea is still at an early stage and you would like to discuss it first before writing a formal book proposal, then please contact us; one of our commissioning editors will get in touch with you.

We're not just looking for published authors; if you have strong technical skills but no writing experience, our experienced editors can help you develop a writing career, or simply get some additional reward for your expertise.

## Mastering Object-oriented Python

ISBN: 978-1-78328-097-1        Paperback: 634 pages

Grasp the intricacies of object-oriented programming in Python in order to efficiently build powerful real-world applications

1.  Create applications with flexible logging, powerful configuration and command-line options, automated unit tests, and good documentation.

2.  Use the Python special methods to integrate seamlessly with built-in features and the standard library.

3.  Design classes to support object persistence in JSON, YAML, Pickle, CSV, XML, Shelve, and SQL.

## Learning Python Data Visualization

ISBN: 978-1-78355-333-4        Paperback: 212 pages

Master how to build dynamic HTML5-ready SVG charts using Python and the pygal library

1.  A practical guide that helps you break into the world of data visualization with Python.

2.  Understand the fundamentals of building charts in Python.

3.  Packed with easy-to-understand tutorials for developers who are new to Python or charting in Python.

Please check **www.PacktPub.com** for information on our titles

Made in the USA
San Bernardino, CA
23 May 2018